What You Already Know & Don't ...

The B2B Sales Playbook

By Aaron Tighe

First published in 2024
www.b2bsalesplaybook.com
knowanddont@gmail.com
© Aaron P. Tighe, 2024

Cataloguing -in-Publication details are available from the National Library of Australia www.librariesaustralia.nla.gov.au

Ebook ISBN: 978-0-9756620-1-4
Printed book ISBN: 978-0-9756620-2-1
Audio book: ISBN: 978-0-9756620-0-7

Printed and bound by IngramSpark

Disclaimer: The material in this publication is in the nature of general comment only, and neither purports nor intends to be advice. Readers should not act on the basis of any matter in this publication without considering (and if appropriate taking) professional advice with due regard to their own particular circumstances. The author and publisher expressly disclaim all and any liability to any person, whether a purchaser of this publication or not, in respect of anything and the consequences done or omitted to be done by any such person in reliance, whether whole or partial, upon the whole or any part of the contents of this publication.

To Julie, Sean, Megan
You are my inspiration always

What a delight it was to read What You Already Know & Don't...
I came away energized and believing even I could succeed in B2B
sales! I can happily say I devoured it cover to cover and LOVED it.
Thanks for the privilege of diving into your creative and powerfully
practical guidebook. THIS BOOK MUST BE PUBLISHED!

*Joseph Michelli – The Author of #1 New York Times Best Sellers: The
Starbucks experience, The New Gold Standard 5 Leadership Principles
for Creating a Legendary Customer Experience Courtesy of The Ritz
Carlton Hotel Company, How to Drive Delight the Mercedes Benz Way.*

CONTENTS

ABOUT THE AUTHOR

FOLLOWING HIS RETIREMENT from professional football at the young age of 22, Aaron has worked in the fields of Business Sales and Business Sales Management for 30 years. He began his sales career in the UK with NTL before moving to Australia in 1999, where he joined the competitive telecommunications industry with Macquarie Technology Group. Aaron has been a spokesperson for the company's Heartbeat program, which won the Gold Winner Award for the 'Best in the World' customer experience program at the World Communications Awards in 2020. Aaron features in New York Times Best Selling Author Joseph Michelli's: Customer Magic, The Macquarie Way. Aaron is also the author of the football-focused autobiography 'What It Takes'. Aaron is married to Julie, and they have two children, Sean, and Megan. He resides in Perth, Western Australia.

INTRODUCTION

IF YOU'RE READING this, chances are, you're immersed in the world of business sales, or contemplating taking that monumental step into the profession. You might even be a procurement specialist, aiming to delve deeper into the sales function to bolster your negotiation skills with vendors. Regardless, before we delve any deeper, allow me to say, "Thank you very much" for choosing this book. This act alone is a profound honour for me. It signifies your perception of value, your willingness to exchange your time and funds. We commence our journey with a sale! My promise is to validate this exchange of value in the following chapters.

I've been fortunate enough to shape a career in professional sales spanning three decades. It wasn't premeditated. As a teenager, I didn't yearn for a career in sales, broadcasting this ambition to my family and friends. Instead, I aspired to become a professional footballer. Fortuitously, I realized this dream, albeit briefly, playing for one of England's top clubs at the time. However, a debilitating injury at 22 prematurely ended my football career. Everything I had dreamed of and dedicated myself to from a young age, literally was broken, having reached a cliff edge with a vast chasm beyond. A primal realization that I needed to find a new profession to survive kicked in.

Many of us in professional sales stumble upon the career serendipitously. Post-football, a football club owner facilitated a role for me in an Accounts Department, assisting the Management Accountants. By age 24, I intuitively discerned that accountancy wasn't my calling. Yet, handling payroll, I observed the hefty commissions earned by the sales team - a staggering 400% more than my earnings. My youthful curiosity pondered, "How do I achieve that?" Pursuing this thought, I uncovered the captivating world of professional sales techniques and skills. This stint in accountancy led me to the realm of sales, journeying from door-to-door residential sales to orchestrating multi-million-dollar B2B sales. Success in sales allowed me to traverse the globe, walk on China's Great Wall, marvel at Cambodia's Angkor Wat temple, sit co-pilot on a sea plane through Halong Bay's cliffs in Vietnam, and be awestruck by San Francisco's Golden Gate Bridge. What experiences await you, or have you already embarked on? One thing is certain: Sales, especially B2B Sales, can yield remarkable rewards for those who sharpen their skills and embody an insatiable drive and tenacity to succeed. It's the catalyst that turns dreams into reality.

Beyond the financial incentives and the tantalizing rewards, the allure of sales lies in its human interaction. The joy of discovering, through personal connections, ways in which you can assist, is unparalleled. When this connection cultivates a business agreement, often blossoming into years of engagement and occasionally friendship, it transforms work into a special endeavour.

We all possess a unique blend of skills, strengths, knowledge, and attributes that enable us to sell our ideas, our solutions, to others. Everyone is at a different stage of this journey. Whether you're a novice or a veteran, it's certain that we don't have all the answers. Even the crème de la crème, the most seasoned, trained, accomplished salespersons in the world, don't. Why? Simply because every new customer interaction is uncharted territory, providing fresh perspectives, challenges, and insights. They are bends in the road, where you're unsure what lies beyond; just that success awaits if you navigate well. That's the magnetism. It's the 'what we don't know' in the title of this book.

As you cultivate your sales career, you'll encounter diverse individuals with varying styles and skills. Instinctively, you'll distinguish the poor from the good, and the good from the great. The lessons in this book draw from a cocktail of extensive reading, attentive listening, and learning from esteemed global sales programs, as well as adopting effective techniques from sales maestros and leaders. Yet, the most significant learnings of what works and what doesn't stem from observing and interacting with the most crucial people you'll engage with - your customers!

This quick 2-hour read is a playbook comprising practical techniques, advice, and anecdotes that contribute to successful professional business sales. Designed with succinct chapters, you can dip in at any point, depending on your needs. Consider this a companion guide, a reference during crucial moments like submitting a proposal and so on.

So, let's commence. Once again, thank you for your time. As salespeople, we're endowed with remarkable communication skills. If these chapters provide even one tip, technique, or skill that you can incorporate into your toolkit, consider it time well-spent. That one insight could spell the difference between a win or loss, or even between a decent career and an extraordinary one that fulfills dreams. Here's to successful selling!

EVERYTHING BOUGHT IS SOLD BY SOMEONE

WHETHER IT'S AN online purchase, a transaction at an upscale shopping mall, a local merchant, a car dealership, or even a corporate boardroom, there's always a driving force persuading you to shift money from your wallet or bank account to another. Generally, we don't give it much thought. We see the value in the item, it satisfies a need or desire we have, and for a fleeting moment, we feel good, content, or occasionally anxious about our bank balance.

A casual remark like, "He was a nice guy," or "She was helpful," may surface, subconsciously acknowledging that the interaction was pleasant, and we'd happily buy again from the same brand, company, store, or even individual. Naturally, the reverse is true as well, and negative experiences such as dealing with a pushy or rude person can deter us from returning to make another purchase unless we have no alternative.

The heart of the purchasing process is human interaction with a salesperson. It's about looking someone in the eye, engaging, and building rapport, or not. We harbour an implicit trust or desire to believe in the person. We think, "I'm doing the right thing," or "Surely, you're not going to let me down." We quickly and effortlessly set aside the notion that the person is merely performing their job, possibly trying to reach a sales quota and employing techniques to help convince us that we genuinely need the item we're contemplating. Being engaged in this process signifies our openness to buying. A bit of guidance from the salesperson, if necessary, seals the deal.

So, where's the human interaction in online purchasing? I'd suggest it's embedded in the journey that leads to that point. Company or product branding/advertising guides you to the online store, and a positive experience there triggers a purchase. Behind the scenes, a team of sales and marketing professionals subtly, or not so subtly, urges you to take the final step. Yet again, we overlook the salespeople involved. We rarely reflect on how our purchase contributes to someone's targets, commissions, bonuses, and overall success. At most, we might leave a comment about our experience in an online survey. Thank you very much!

So, the reality is that every purchase has a salesperson behind it, regardless of the title you assign to that person: Account Manager, Account Executive, Business Development Manager, Marketing Manager, Shop Assistant, Real Estate Agent, VP, President, Managing Director, CEO, and so forth. It's widely acknowledged that human interaction boosts sales—that's a given. While seamless integration with an online transactional experience is crucial in many business-to-consumer and business-to-business sales interactions, it's the people who keep the sales world spinning. Without that human touch in sales, a business's products remain static, failing to find a home. Hats off to all Salespeople!

In summary:

> ➤ Human interaction with salespeople influences buying behaviour.
> ➤ Even an online sale involves a human who has influenced your decision to buy.
> ➤ People are the force that drives the business sales world.

THE PERSONALITY OF A SALESPERSON

ISN'T EVERYONE A salesperson in some sense? Unless we live on a desert island with no other living person, the reality is that we learn skills from the earliest age, that help us to engage with other human beings. Why? Well simply we need them to serve our own needs for basic survival, safety, love, relationships, recognition and doing what we want to do*. Without the ability to communicate clearly, showing; empathy, assertion, emotion, understanding, gratitude, trust, fortitude, we'd be cast aside, left to our own devices on a metaphorical desert island. So, what do we do? We sell ourselves and our value to others in return for helping with our needs. Most of the time completely unaware of what we are doing. It's just an instinctive human behaviour.

Think of a time when you were young, and you wanted something from your parents or siblings and got it. How did you go about it? how did you ask? Were you meek, shy, did you cry a little, show you were upset? or were you a little pushy, assertive, demanding? Maybe you asked months in advance, planting the seeds for the birthday or Christmas present. I'm sure you created some magic right? There you go! you were selling! However, it is true that not everyone's personality traits are geared to being outstanding dedicated salespeople, skilled to the level that a business will demand, to achieve financial targets. Yes, we all sell in some way but what personality traits are needed to make it a profession? and more importantly a profession as an invaluable top performer? Here are key attributes:

- Self-Drive – When you are around a gun salesperson, they ooze this. It's in their eyes, body language, voice, and emotion. There is a metaphorical goal line, and they instinctively are driving to get across it. I once had a CEO describe it as "eye of the tiger", they know what they want to achieve and are compelled to get there, bashing, and knocking obstacles out of the way to win.

- Individualisation – The top salespeople have an innate ability to want to understand where the other person is coming from, what they want, need, what will make them feel good, satisfied, and happy with the outcome, all along intrinsically meshing the value of their solution to that need. It is a beautiful skill to watch in action when done well. It's a real human connection, a meeting of minds.

- Ambivert – The traditional view of salespeople needing to be extroverts is somewhat accurate but not entirely. By their nature extroverts love being with people, communicating, sharing their thoughts openly, being the centre of the room. They also have an ability to speak almost without thinking, such is the speed of cognitive interpreting of thought to then verbalise a response. This is a useful attribute in selling, 'thinking on your feet' as it were. On the contrary, if it's too one sided on the speaking side, salespeople will be seen as 'too talkative', 'can't shut them up', 'arrogant', 'they don't listen' etc. We've all seen it, heard it, experienced that type of selling. One challenge is: if the purchaser is an introvert, they'll very quickly tune out and feel uncomfortable with the onslaught. Being a chameleon whereby you can move between the benefits of extraversion and introversion is a massive advantage. It links to individualisation and showing that understanding of the other person, the balancing of speaking, active listening, considered, albeit quick thinking compelling communications with the person.

- Optimistic – Think about buying from someone who is negative about the product, solution, day, or life in general. Feel that energy. It's not good, is it? You might buy the product but you're not going to want to go back there in a hurry, are you? Now think the converse, buying from someone who is smiling, has a pleasant energy. upbeat in their verbal language, body language and tone. You can feel your energy lift and feel good! That is who you want to be in every engagement with customers, the optimist, the bright person that people will want to engage and be with. If your mind isn't in that optimistic, positive state, you'll need to work on changing to that state. Saying in a fast punchy way "Energy, energy, energy" is my quick mental mantra. Physical action like punching the air or doing something that gets the blood flowing is also helpful. We need to be up mentally to get the best out of ourselves and in doing so, this reflects on others. Sales comes with plenty of no's, losses and deals not coming in. That's the game. Great salespeople: learn, see the positives, and move on, quickly looking for a new opportunity, saying: "Next!"

- Persistent – There's an itch that you just have to scratch until its done itching. That's what this trait is like. You are going to keep asking, emailing, calling, texting, anyone that is going to help you in your task to win over a customer, or reach a sales target, or incentive. You are steadfast in making it happen in the short or long term. Being professionally consistent in your approach is important; Always polite. courteous, on-time when you say you will follow up. I recall a customer CEO once telling my Boss in a meeting that "I can set my clock by him, he'll always call when he says he will". That doesn't happen by accident; you need to make sure you have a good reminder system in place. For me it was plain old excel with notes against dates. Whether its email/calendar or the multitude of apps you can use as reminders, get in a habit of tracking and planning reminders, and act on time.

These were the words of a Product Manager I worked with, as he described his reasons for selecting a vendor "In the end I just went ok, the business is yours you've shown the most tenacity". He continued: ""initially I didn't have that vendor shortlisted, I had other more well-known brands in mind, but this sales rep just kept ringing me, asking for the chance to prove themselves. Eventually, I just went "Ok, come and meet me." Post presentation he smashed the other salespeople on chasing me and showing his enthusiasm. There wasn't much between the vendors and eventually, his eagerness and passion won me over; we signed off with him"". Without a doubt the persistence and enthusiasm of the Sales guy in this story won over the Product Manager. I love this story. It's not just the big brands that can win, it really showed how people make the difference.

- Knowledge –"Let me get back to you on that", "I don't know ",," I need to speak with my manager". Have you ever been on the receiving end of one of those conversations with a Salesperson? The one where you seem to know more than them; or when you ask advice, you can see by their fumbling that they simply don't have good knowledge. It's not necessarily a dampener on the experience of buying, depending on the circumstance; however, it does set the Pro's aside from the Amateurs. Customers want to deal with someone who will provide them with insights, lessons and in turn knowledge they can use in their buying decisions. The top salespeople will 'knowledge up'. They'll get to know the solution and how it benefits a customer. They'll get to know the industry, the competition's position. You don't have to be a technical expert or a specialist in a specific area if those members are part of the sales team. However, you do need to be able to articulate confidently your excellent level of knowledge in the solution you are asking them to buy.

Barbara was a consistent No.1 performing Account Executive for a national IT company with a portfolio of existing business accounts to manage and sell to. She had over 6 years of experience in the industry and built-up rapport with her customers by having knowledge to answer 90% of their questions on the spot. Customers loved her because she was efficient. They knew they could call or meet and get answers straight away. Barbara would use other customer examples from her history to bring her knowledge to life. She was also keen to, every month, provide updates from the industry on what was new, what they could take advantage of to save money or increase productivity. She would also, skilfully position, support technical personnel in meetings with customers, to expand to the customer a broader level of knowledge. She was consciously demonstrating to the customer that she could help them by tapping into a larger pool of knowledge. As a customer, having that level of Account Executive provides you with comfort that they have you covered.

- Confidence - The sword of Excalibur for salespeople. Think of a recent large purchase you made, one that involved interaction with the vendors Salesperson. It could be a house, car, holiday etc. What was their demeanour? Were they shy with minimal eye contact? Did they seem unsure in their communications? No! I expect they were the opposite right? Confidence is a wonderful trait. It gives you a great chance to build rapport with the buyer when shown naturally. Even if you are not on your best form or not feeling confident, avoid displaying that emotion to a customer. In that circumstance, prime before the meeting and get into a state of professional confidence.

Tony worked in the highly competitive tourism sector. Tony was what is called a 'lone wolf salesman'. He didn't mix with the other sales team members, kept himself to himself, was not outwardly showy in any way but was a consistent high performer, always at the top of the league tables for sales. He was the best dressed by a mile: dark grey suit, tie, white collar, tie clip, long black winter cashmere coat. His short dark hair, combed back, Elvis like, was never out of place. He walked with purpose and when he was talking to you, fixed you with a look that, even without words compelled you to agree with his 'jedi like' mind trick of "you will buy". Tony oozed confidence, in his look and his language. He made sure he knew enough about the solutions to work a sale himself and was to the heavier scale of assertiveness in convincing customers. After a couple of years of earning good money, Tony saw changes to the commission plans as damaging to his pocket and moved on. He knew what he wanted, needed, and was calculating in his methods.

I tell this story to show the power of appearing and being confident in your approach. For me Tony was successful because his confidence was so convincing. He didn't have the other key skills considered by some as necessary to be in the top 20% of elite sales-manship like: empathy, individualisation, team-player, but he was still a consistent top performer and very convincing at that.

In summary:

- Everyone is a Salesperson in their life to get what they need/want.
- Self-Drive, Individualisation, Ambivert, Optimism, Persistence, Knowledge, Confidence are key personality traits for top hitters in sales.
- Confidence – Always show it when engaging with customers. Prime your state physically and mentally. People buy from confident people.

PLAY 1.
CREATE A WINNING FORMULA

A LITTLE PREPARATION GOES A LONG WAY

"HOW'S BUSINESS?" "WHAT'S your role?" "What does your company do?" You'll often hear these questions from salespeople when they're interacting with potential or existing customers. Stop for a moment and reflect. What's missing in this approach? There's nothing inherently wrong with these questions if you're content with being average. But what if we reframed these inquiries?

How about this: "I noted from the Chairman's recent address that the business is…" or "I understand that you've been in role X for the past Y years…" or "I'm intrigued by your focus on these particular products/services; can you elaborate?"

Can you discern the distinct difference between these approaches? Which one do you think leaves a customer feeling understood and catered to? Much like you have goals, targets, and passions, so do your customers. When you connect with these interests, you foster deeper, more insightful conversations that align with their priorities. By dedicating time to research the industry, company, role, and the individual, you're more likely to make a positive impression during your initial and subsequent interactions. Key insights to arm yourself with include:

a. **Company structure and specifics** – Are they public, private, national, global? What's their location, employee count, and financial status?

a. **Their unique selling proposition** – What key messages are they using to differentiate themselves from competitors?

a. **Their offerings** – What solutions, products, or services do they provide?

a. **Individual insights** – What's their work history, interests, and connections? Ensure you pronounce their name correctly, demonstrating sincere interest in them as individuals.

The digital world is a treasure trove of information for the diligent sales professional. Look out for:

- Executive commentary in annual reports
- Company newsletters
- Website updates
- Industry forums
- News articles
- LinkedIn company posts
- AI tools like Open Systems Chat GPT, Bard
- Information on LinkedIn about the individual and business
- Social connections to your acquaintances

Using your research to establish connections can pave the way for warm introductions. This approach could involve colleagues, customers, friends, or even Executives and Board members. A typical warm approach might sound like, "I noticed you worked with our Executive John at your former company. I would appreciate the opportunity to introduce myself and our business…"

There's no excuse for not being prepared and knowledgeable when conversing with a customer. Schedule your preparation time – don't leave it for the car ride or the reception area. However, avoid overdoing it. You must strike a balance. It's counterproductive to spend days researching one customer with a low potential return. Be knowledgeable enough to demonstrate your understanding of their business and how your experience and company align with their needs.

Imagine a championship boxing match. Your chances of success increase significantly if you've studied your opponent's movements and techniques in advance.

Sue was the Account Executive for a large soft drinks manufacturer. She was attempting to convince a national retailer to stock and sell their soft drink. Sue had arranged a meeting with the retailer's Procurement Manager. Rather than simply showing up to the meeting and presenting her PowerPoint presentation, Sue prepared two days in advance.

She researched the company's latest financial report, picking up on the key focus areas from the Chairman and CEO's statements. Sue then researched independent news on the web and third-party consultant papers on the retailer's industry. She entered the contact's name into LinkedIn, got familiar with their background, and identified other individuals likely to be involved in the retailer's purchasing decisions. With a summary of notes captured on her laptop, Sue then sent the summary internally to Managers and Executives to seek out anyone who might have valuable intelligence on the retailer's contacts and/or business. You never know, an inside friendly contact may be available. Sue completed one hour of prep work for a potential opportunity that could fulfill her quarterly target. That's right! One hour! Not a day or a week, just one hour.

Sue attended the meeting and, three months later, secured a major national contract. When asked why they had selected Sue's business over their competitors, the retailer replied, "It was the solution fit, and Sue and her team were the only ones who really demonstrated that they understood our business." That message of understanding all started with Sue's preparation.

In summary:

> ➤ Research your customers' company and the individuals you're meeting before your interaction.
> ➤ Find a common link that personalizes the engagement.
> ➤ Utilize online resources to gain insights into their business and backgrounds.
> ➤ Schedule time for research and preparation. Knowledge is power.
> ➤ Strike a balance – don't go overboard with preparation.

PROSPECTING FOR APPOINTMENTS AND OPPORTUNITIES

"THE LEADS ARE weak," the sales character complains to the Boss in the classic movie Glengarry Glen Ross. "The F...... leads are weak! You're weak!" the Boss fires back. It's an uncomfortable, cringe-inducing moment in the film: the well-intentioned underdog lambasted by the ruthless city slicker brought in to rev up the sales team. While fictional, this scene reflects a common reality across sales teams throughout time. There are invariably team members who miss their targets, quotas, and incentives and resort to a defensive mantra of "it's not my fault." They point fingers elsewhere. Here are some common scapegoats:

- "I get no leads."
- "I get all the low-quality leads."
- "Marketing is useless."
- "I have the least promising territory."
- "Everything has already been sold."
- "Customers are not interested."
- "I've engaged them before; there's no opportunity."
- "The targets are set too high."
- "The others just got lucky."

It's all too easy to fall into this trap of excuse-making, turning it into a psychological shield against disappointment and defeat, thereby convincing ourselves that lagging in sales performance is not our fault. However, top performers understand and persistently apply the principle of diligent prospecting, creating a stream of opportunities that guarantee their success. The adage, "It's a numbers game," holds true. Whether you're highly skilled or a novice, whether your closing ratio is 1:1 or 100:1, maintaining a consistent flow of opportunities above your closing ratio ensures you hit your targets.

The farming analogy of sowing seeds in one field while harvesting in another aptly describes sales success. One field represents new opportunity creation, while the other symbolizes the proposing and closing of the sales process, regardless of the outcome. Both fields demand equal attention and enthusiasm. Neglect one, and you'll experience a drought period due to either a shortage of opportunities or a poor sales closing rate.

With the development of technology and support systems, we've seen various prospecting methodologies rise and fall. Door-to-door sales, cold calling, exhibition stands, networking events, mail-outs, and social media have all been prime ways to build a prospective sales pipeline. As we move into the era of AI, innovations will empower salespeople to define a target market and create tailored campaigns in mere seconds, as opposed to hours or days. This is yet another method, not an ultimate solution.

Is there one miraculous method, one solution to every sales-person's prayer? Yes, and it's called 'whatever it takes.' This simply means to utilize every available method. In the upcoming chapter '90 and 180 Days Out Pipeline,' we will delve deeper into the importance of consistency in your selling.

David and Joe, two business sales team members at a medical equipment manufacturer, have both been with the company for 24 months. They sell to health centres and hospitals. Over the past year, David consistently hit 100% + of his monthly quota, while Joe struggled with inconsistent wins, achieving only 50% in the same period. "I have a really poor territory," Joe laments. "Everything's been sold, and I'm spending all my time handling operational issues. I don't have any time for selling."

David's perspective is quite different. "I'm relentlessly working all of the contacts in my territory. I make it a point to meet them weekly, building rapport and immediately responding to their needs, especially when they encounter problems. This is fostering trust, and they're naturally reordering from me. Moreover, I'm receiving quality referrals from these contacts into other areas of the health centres, which is expanding my opportunities."

In this example, David assumes responsibility, consistently nurturing contacts, opportunities, and referrals. His positive attitude, laser-focused on what he needs to do to succeed, has him managing sales orders while simultaneously building new opportunities through repeat business and new contacts. Conversely, Joe is trapped in a blame game, risking a downward spiral. Of course, there will be instances when a salesperson's opportunities are stifled for specific reasons. However, this should not be a consistent excuse. Underperformance is exposed when others in the team are succeeding.

In summary:

- ➤ Avoid falling into the trap of excuses and blaming others.
- ➤ Exceptional salespeople assume full responsibility for their performance and results.
- ➤ Always sow seeds in one field while harvesting in another to prevent opportunity droughts.
- ➤ Utilize all available methods for prospecting. Do whatever it takes to build success.

YOUR OWN DEDICATED EVENTS

I HAVE A good friend who has been in the hospitality industry for over 30 years, shucking fresh oysters at top-notch restaurants and private events in Australia. He has worked globally, and his career longevity speaks volumes. Walking into his restaurant or function, you're guaranteed to feel valued as he exclaims, "Hey, the Tighe's have arrived; Everyone, the Tighe's are here!" He makes a fuss, remembers your name, looks you in the eyes, and provides his undivided attention. Throughout the evening, he periodically checks in, ensuring you're comfortable, and introduces you to other guests. For many years, I've seen him make people feel special. It's not necessarily the food (although the oysters are exceptional!), the restaurant's ambiance, or the bill that leaves a lasting impression, but the 'EXPERIENCE', the emotional impact. It creates a memorable event that you'll return to and share with your friends.

The term 'event' can conjure various interpretations. In the context of business sales, I propose events can range from intimate round table discussions on specific topics for 6 to 16 participants, to larger presentation-style gatherings spotlighting your business's solutions. Add to this list, purely social gatherings that mix customers and prospects.

So, what are you aiming to achieve by hosting an event that draws in customers and prospects? Ultimately, you want them to buy from you and continue to do so. So, what should be your focal point? As in one-to-one selling, the answer lies in understanding the customer's needs and wants and guiding them towards your proposed solution. But, what more can you do? The answer is "Make them feel good."

People 'feel good' at an event when they learn something new or consolidate their thoughts by hearing others speak. It's innate for us to desire growth and learning, and events can facilitate this. Over the years, I've been a strong advocate for roundtable discussions with diverse industries and roles, where people discuss topics over a meal. The positive feedback from customers who walk away with new acquaintances and insights to incorporate into their business is always rewarding.

With this objective in mind, whether it's an event you've personally orchestrated or one your business has arranged to generate new sales opportunities, focus on the customer 'experience'.

- Before the event, ensure all key contacts are on the invite list. Can you give each of them a personal call, making it a personal invitation?
- At the event, make sure each customer feels welcome, is introduced to others, and is involved in sharing or learning insights.
- After the event, express gratitude for their attendance, follow up, check in, and schedule a meeting to discuss the topic(s) further.

It's easy to consider events as the responsibility of others, such as the marketing department or an event manager. However, as a salesperson, the accountability lies with you. Events provide a vehicle for you to invite your customers and prospects. It's like operating a bus for a couple of hours, going from point A to B. It's your responsibility to ensure your guests board the bus and have a fantastic experience while aboard and afterwards. Depending on their experience, they may decide to ride again, possibly bringing friends, or they might choose another bus next time. We certainly don't want the latter!

Julia is a sales representative for an IT software company. She has developed a solid reputation with her customers over her three years in the role. Despite various attempts, Julia has been unable to secure appointments with a key new target account. She contemplates leveraging her excellent customer relationships to gain traction with the target account. After researching their business, she learns that innovation via new technology is part of their 5-year strategy. Julia organizes a roundtable breakfast for six guests, focusing on sharing insights about implementing tech innovations. She specifically highlights a high-profile customer, whose experience she knows will resonate with the attendees.

Her next step is coordinating with the marketing department to develop a compelling invitation for targeted guests. Once prepared, she forwards the invite to the guest list and follows up individually with a personal call asking them to attend. Upon calling the new account target and explaining the attendee list, the executive accepts. This acceptance opens the door for Julia to begin a conversation with them for the first time. During the event, Julia facilitates the discussions. The executive is impressed by the calibre of the attendees, the insightful conversation, and the positive reviews of Julia's services from the guests. Julia follows up after the event with an initial meeting with the executive and his team to explore potential opportunities. Ten months later, the first order is received, and a new customer relationship is established.

In summary:

- ➢ Organize customer events that cater to their needs and interests.
- ➢ Make your events memorable by making attendees feel good.
- ➢ Assume responsibility for arranging and attending events; don't delegate it to others. Be in control of your customer interactions.

REFERRAL

SALESPEOPLE WHO OVERCOME the awkwardness of soliciting referrals will find their pipeline quality improving, ultimately closing more deals. There is nothing like a warm introduction. Place yourself in the shoes of the buyer. You've just had a great experience with the company, product, and salesperson, perhaps over multiple occasions. On a rating out of ten, you score them 10. The salesperson asks you, "Hey, thank you for being our customer, I really appreciate it. Is there anyone you can think of that would also like our service/product/solution? It really helps if we get a warm intro." What's your reaction? In most cases, I reckon it's, "Sure, let me think, perhaps try this person, that person." If the experience of the buyer is really positive, they will be happy to refer. There is nothing scary or uncomfortable in that. It's how the world works; we like to help others and good people.

Consistent application of this approach means that every sale could lead to further introductions and opportunities, allowing you to grow your network through referrals. Consider this example in a business sale context:

You secure an account. The buyer provides two contacts. You reach out to the two contacts. Both agree to meet over coffee because they trust the mutual connection. One meeting progresses as the timing is perfect and aligns with their buying cycle. The other meeting goes well, but the timing isn't quite right. You agree to follow up and meet later in the year, which you schedule in your calendar. By merely asking for referrals, you now have two entirely new pipeline opportunities, one short-term and one long-term.

Boldly asking for referrals, whether the individual has made a purchase or not, can be an excellent habit to cultivate. Every interaction with a customer, partner, or prospect presents a chance to discover a new contact and opportunity. It's common to hear salespeople dismiss meetings or opportunities as a "waste of time." This perspective is valid only if you were looking for an immediate sale and nothing more. Did you ask for, and receive, any referrals, any connections to new contacts, or future opportunities? If so, kudos to you! Particularly in business sales, the first attempt might not win, but it can position you favourably for the next time they're in the market, leaving a positive impression.

Once a referral leads to success, it's crucial to acknowledge and thank the original referrer. Sending a personalized thank-you gift or note, not only leaves a good impression on the referrer but also reinforces your relationship. Who knows, you might just receive more referrals!

Mohammad is the top Business Development Manager for a global office furniture business. He has maintained the No.1 position in the sales team for five consecutive years. His secret? Mohammad shares, "I've made it a habit to ask for introductions and connections from almost everyone I interact with. I extend this approach to new employees in our company, asking them about their past work experiences and networks. If there's a potential match, I request them to connect me, and I handle the rest. I follow the same practice with customers, ex-customers, alliances, and friends. Warm introductions have been invaluable, consistently generating new conversations, meetings, and opportunities. As my connections grow, my network expands. It's like a snowball rolling downhill—it just keeps getting bigger."

In summary:

- ➤ Overcome the discomfort of asking for referrals.
- ➤ Request referrals from both buyers and non-buyers.
- ➤ Personally acknowledge and thank referrers.

PICK UP THE PHONE AND RING

IN HIS BOOK, "Fanatical Prospecting" (highly recommended), Jeb Blount asserts, "The telephone is, has always been, and will continue to be the most powerful sales prospecting tool." He continues, "The brutal truth is this: salespeople who ignore the phone fail. They deliver mediocre results and cheat themselves out of hard-earned cash."

Indeed, phone prospecting can provoke that innate fear of rejection. You might imagine, "The ground will open up, and the bats of hell will carry me away to my doom!" However, consider this:

If you avoid calling prospects and your sales numbers dwindle, those bats may find you regardless!

Isn't it better to call and seek a potential meeting or opportunity, rather than avoid the call and live with the illusion of safety?

Don't overanalyse it! If you find yourself saying, "I'm not prepared enough," "They won't answer at this time," "I'll call later, after dealing with this email," or "They probably won't be interested, I'll just email them," you're falling into the trap of avoidance. Your mind aims to protect you from the sting of rejection, but the key is not to dwell on the potential negatives—just act. Set a target, focus, and follow through.

Allocating specific time to prepare for calls is essential. Gaining some understanding of the prospects' industries, businesses, or personal needs to reference during the call will help build rapport. Use the plethora of online tools to glean insights swiftly before making the call. Preparation shouldn't be an excuse for procrastination, though; keep it brief, then make the call.

Reflecting on my early sales role as a 25-year-old selling telecoms fibre/cable in the UK, I learned the importance of concise, purposeful conversation. The pitch had to be quick and decisive, just like on a phone call. You're taking up someone's time, and they want you to get to the point. A meandering, uncertain delivery will only lead to frustration and a premature end to the call.

So, what does an effective business phone call look like? Here's a generic example:

"Hi Bill, this is Aaron from Company Z. I've noticed in a recent news article that your company is focusing on cost reduction this year. We've recently helped a customer reduce costs by 15% with our Solution Y. Could we schedule a brief introductory meeting next Tuesday or Friday?"

Breaking it down, this approach:

a. Introduces you and your company.

a. States a researched need of the customer.

a. Provides a relevant example of how you can help.

a. Requests a meeting, providing options for the appointment time.

Remember, the goal is to arrange a face-to-face meeting, not to make a sale over the phone. Gather information about the prospect's buying cycle to ensure you reach out at an opportune time.

Joel and Leo are six months into their new sales roles at a steel manufacturing/distribution business. Joel is organised, setting out his diary to ensure he has a daily research slot and a time for outbound calling. He aims to reach key decision-makers/influencers, so he adjusts his calling times to circumvent the customers' likely busy periods. He does his research from 9:30-10:30 a.m. and alternates his daily calls between 11:00 a.m.-12:00 p.m. and 4:30-5:30 p.m. Why the separation of these activities? It allows Joel to concentrate solely on the specific skills needed for each. Research thinking and actions don't distract him from picking up the phone and calling each prospect. It's crucial for him to remain in that zone as any excuse to avoid making the calls could arise. The variation in calling times, between late morning and late afternoon, improves his chances of making contact. Between these core periods, he schedules meetings, emails, and proposal preparation.

On the other hand, Leo decides on his daily approach as he starts his day. First, he checks and responds to his emails. Then, he prepares proposals and quotes for customer meetings, which is always a rush against time. He reluctantly attends any team meetings, often muttering to himself and others, "Who has time for these?" Whenever there's a gap, Leo looks up a potential client to call, finds them on LinkedIn, sends a connection request, and congratulates himself! Too busy to research and make another call, he returns to emails and follow-ups with clients.

So, who do you think has built a better pipeline and consistently finds new opportunities from outbound calling? Correct, it's Joel! He's transformed it into a daily habit, a ritual of outbound success. It's a priority for him because he knows that without such discipline and efficiency, his sales numbers would suffer. Leo, however, is leaving it to chance, always thinking, "One day, I'll do it," or consciously understanding that there will always be an excuse not to make outbound calls. Indeed, he thinks, "I'll always have an escape."

In summary:

➢ Phone call prospecting is critical for sales success. Neglect it at your peril.
➢ Avoid overthinking. Act!
➢ Dedicate regular, fixed times for preparation and calls.
➢ Craft a personalized message that will resonate.
➢ Aim for a meeting, keeping the call brief and pointed.
➢ If prospects are not currently in a buying cycle, note when they will be for future

EMAIL

WHEN WAS THE last time you opened an email from an unknown individual or corporation? It's likely been quite a while, hasn't it? We are often overwhelmed by emails and fixated on ticking off our daily to-do list, leaving us little motivation to explore an unfamiliar cold or spam email. It's probable that you promptly delete it or direct it to your junk or clutter folders. If you're a salesperson, you might believe that dispatching a flurry of emails will help you meet your sales goals. However, this notion is largely whimsical. You may feel accomplished, but in reality, you've simply convinced yourself that pressing a few keys and hearing the imaginary sound of an email being sent constitutes hard work.

Incorporating email into your strategy needs to be done in conjunction with another method, as a subsequent step. Here are a few possibilities:

- **Phone Call** - After the initial phone call, regardless of whether you've spoken to the customer, secured an appointment or not, an email containing brief, relevant insight can be effective. If the customer is in the buying cycle, they may delve into your material or investigate your offering online.

- **Event** - Thanking attendees for their participation, adding a personal touch about meeting them there and providing insightful follow-up material is recommended.
- **Referral** - Similar to the phone call approach, you're gradually establishing your narrative with the person through an email that strengthens your case for a meeting. It's important not to default to sending an email - make the call first.
- **Digital Campaign** - If your marketing team has detected that the contact is demonstrating interest through website visits or interaction with digital campaign content, a strategic email linked to the campaign with a meeting request might be timely.
- **Meeting** - Following up any meetings, whether initial or ongoing, with a summary of the discussions and next steps, is a professional courtesy. Make it a habit to do so immediately on the same day, while the details are fresh and before other distractions set in.

If your objective is to secure a meeting through the email, remember to request one in a professional and polite manner. Don't hold back.

An effective email structure could be as follows:

o A headline that captures the customer's attention and is relevant to them.

o A warm, genuine opening sentence that, if possible, contains a personal touch. This could be based on information you've gathered about the person through research or from a previous meeting.

- o A sentence that ties into the headline, demonstrating your understanding of their challenge or need.
- o A proposal on how your solution can help address their challenge or need.
- o A request for a meeting to discuss further or to achieve whatever follow-up action you are aiming for.

Charlotte is the Personal Assistant to the CEO of a Bio-Tech company. She understands that, as a PA, certain email approaches from vendors seeking a meeting with her boss catch her eye and are worthy of attention.

Charlotte's boss, Jane, asks her to set up a meeting with the CEO of a potential buyer. Considering the approach, Charlotte remembers that the two CEOs recently attended an industry innovation speaking event together. This provides a warm connection for the introduction. The potential buyer's CEO has also been in the press recently, discussing growth opportunities in overseas markets. Armed with these two pieces of knowledge, Charlotte crafts her email:

Subject: RE: CEO Meeting – Overseas Expansion

Dear Stephen,

Jane, our CEO, recently spoke with you at the Industry Innovation Conference, which she mentioned was a great success.

Having noticed in the media that overseas markets are a key focus for you this year, Jane has asked me to reach out to arrange a suitable time to meet. Jane has extensive industry knowledge in this area.

Jane is available on the 10th of April at 10am or the 15th of April at 4pm. Do either of these times work for you?

Regards,

Charlotte – Personal Assistant to the CEO

Notice how the subject line relates to something that is known to be of interest to Stephen, the CEO. There is a warm connection in the fact that they spoke together at the event, followed by a reason for Stephen to meet Jane, and a call to action. The email is concise and to the point. It provides just enough information to spark interest. The goal is for the meeting to be the place where knowledge is shared.

In Summary:

> Email cold sales approaches are rarely read or acted on.
> Beware of thinking you've done a great job today because you sent some emails.
> Use emails effectively in conjunction with other customer engagements.
> Construct emails that will grab quick attention with personalised tie ins to the customer.

SOCIAL MEDIA SELLING

"NEVER MAKE ANOTHER cold call" escaped the mouths of some sales trainers pushing the merits of social media channels such as Facebook and LinkedIn as the rise and surge of these platforms took over the world. Oh, the dream! Imagine that as a Salesperson, you build your network on LinkedIn and Facebook, sit back, and let the leads and orders roll in.

The reality, however, is markedly different. If you're banking on meeting your sales goals exclusively via social media outreach, you're likely in for a long wait. Why so? It boils down to the mindset with which most people approach social media. Reflect on it for a moment: Why do you update your Facebook page, post on LinkedIn, or refresh your status? In most instances, it's to connect with friends or colleagues, flaunt an accomplishment, share knowledge, or feel a sense of significance. And, yes, who doesn't relish the surge of satisfaction from the comments, views, and likes they've received?

So, when a salesperson interrupts this sphere with a sales pitch or meeting request, how different does it feel from receiving a spam email or generic direct mail? Not so much, right? It's just another disruption on a different platform. While navigating social media, we're not on a shopping spree or scouting new services for our business; we're in our world of self-promotion and connectivity. My point? Social media isn't a silver bullet for sales; it's merely another tool that can bolster your brand and contribute to the overall impression a buyer has of you.

The days of initiating contact or attending a meeting without any background knowledge on the individual you're meeting should be behind us. The web is usually teeming with information. For one-to-one business networking, tools like LinkedIn and LinkedIn Navigator are invaluable in getting up to speed with your contacts and familiarizing yourself with individuals you're pursuing or have already engaged with. Here are some features and benefits that can enhance your positioning:

- **The contact's history** – This information is invaluable for discovering shared experiences, conversation starters, and understanding their skill set. It facilitates quick rapport building. Everyone appreciates recognition of their accomplishments, whether they express it or not. Remember not to go overboard. A single reference comment in an initial conversation works wonders. For example, "I see, Jim, that you spent five years at X company. Congratulations on your success there. How was that experience?"
- **Shared contacts** – An introduction feels warmer if you can name-drop a mutual contact. Example: "Hi, Joe, I see you are connected with John from X. John suggested I reach out to you directly for an intro. Are you available to meet next week on Monday at 10 am or Tuesday at 3 pm?"

- **The contact's post/article history** – This also is a great way to understand a person's interests and perhaps find some common ground or a discussion point.

Liz is an experienced Business Sales Account Director. She's moved to a start-up finance software company and is tasked with creating new opportunities for the business. Liz has developed over 500 business connections on social media. As part of her strategy, she targets four large businesses a day to research and approach on social media. This will result in 20 a week and 80 a month.

Step 1: Liz researches each company and maps out their organizational chart, starting from the board and executive team and continuing with finance and IT managers or influencers.

Step 2: Liz's research reveals that their CIO is a first connection with the CIO of a former customer, who she knows will recommend her. She also notes that he attended the same university as one of the start-up founders. Bingo! Liz has two warm connections to approach with a message on the social platform.

Step 3: First, Liz contacts her former customer and enquires about the CIO and how they know each other. She also asks if she can mention his name in an introduction. He tells her that they are in the same bike club and are friendly, and he has no problem with her mentioning his name. Great result!

Second, Liz checks in with her founder about the university connection. There is no direct connection; however, the founder lets her know that they are bound to have mutual connections, so it is good to mention it.

Step 4: Liz reaches out on the social platform with a brief message to see if she can connect, to warm the approach:

"Hi Daniel, I'm reaching out to connect. I was recently in touch with the CIO, James, of ABC Ltd who is a customer. He mentioned that he knew you and is happy to recommend me as a contact. I believe you're in the same bike club together. Also, I see that you attended the same university as our founder, Alex. Small world. Thank you, Liz."

A day later, Liz receives a notice that the CIO has connected. Great, this means that he will be aware of posts and information she places on the platform. She notes to follow up with a phone call in a couple of weeks to set up a meeting with the founder, Alex. The university connection will be useful. Liz also plans to invite him to an upcoming event with the friendly customer, James.

In this approach, as you can see, the goal is purely to connect, not to secure an immediate appointment or to sign an immediate contract. You're simply knocking on the person's door, showing them who you are, establishing familiarity and connection. It's about raising their awareness of you and your business. Notice also that Liz hasn't asked the recommender to make the introduction. She has controlled the messaging.

In summary:

- People use social media for networking, business, self-promotion, and learning from influencers or leaders in their field.
- Social media is another tool in the kit bag, not the be-all and end-all.
- Use social platforms to demonstrate your values.
- Platforms like LinkedIn are an excellent way to research and build knowledge to help establish rapport with customers.

ALLIANCES

THERE CAN BE various reasons for forming and leveraging alliances with other companies to help sell your solution. Here we are talking about two companies with distinct products/services working in tandem, as opposed to channel selling, where organizations wholesale or sell through a channel partner.

One main reason is to align products/services to provide a comprehensive solution to customers' needs. For instance, your business might only be able to offer part of the solution, and without a partner, you risk losing out to competitors that provide the full package. Many customers prefer a "one-stop-shop," as the saying goes. However, if you can demonstrate that working with specialists in their unique fields is superior to getting lost among multiple departments of a massive provider, you can present an attractive option. This particularly holds true when the customer is already receiving subpar service from a large provider.

Another crucial reason is referrals and introductions - Alliances can function as an extension of your workforce. They serve as lead generators and field representatives, informing you of potential opportunities. These partnerships can be incentive-based or operate on a "quid pro quo" basis. With the latter, it's a two-way street;

you need to trust their offering with respect to your customers for you to refer them.

For business sales, having regular, open conversations with your partner and sharing knowledge is priceless. What's occurring in your customer base? What's happening in theirs? How can you collaborate with customer x? By doing this, you effectively broaden your network and influence beyond your independent reach. Identifying the right angles from each other to promote is crucial. You will have your independent spheres to work in, and working together can be compelling to customers when executed well.

Marco is an Account Director for a mineral resources company. Asserting the quality of the minerals he sells is essential to gaining an edge over competitors. He meets with Dimitri, an Account Representative for a global quality assurance firm, with whom he regularly exchanges notes. They identify an immediate opportunity with an upcoming large global tender being released by a company that neither currently serves.

They strategize their approach. Dimitri can endorse the quality assurance of Marco's product in their submission, and Marco can recommend Dimitri's quality assurance services to the prospect. The combined strength of the two entities backing each other is more potent than either alone. This straightforward but effective approach leads to a successful bid. Marco secures a new account, complete with an essential stamp of approval for quality. Eight months later, Dimitri's quality assurance business is invited in for a new project by the prospect. Those initial coffee chats have certainly paid off!

In summary:

> ➢ Combine forces with another company's sales representative to provide a more comprehensive customer solution.
> ➢ Meet regularly and strategize jointly.
> ➢ Collaboratively gain referrals and introductions.

90 AND 180 DAYS OUT PIPELINE

"I'M STRUGGLING THIS month, Boss. Despite my attempts to close deals, I'm not receiving responses and customer X needs more time. I'll make up for it next month."

What's the issue with this common exchange? This tense conversation between a Salesperson and their Manager typically stems from the uncomfortable fact that they haven't sold enough. Is it due to a deficiency in closing sales or perhaps a lacklustre attitude towards their job? Possibly...

However, a more likely and prevalent issue is they haven't cultivated sufficient opportunities within the previous 90 to 180 days. In business sales, customers' buying process generally takes 90 days or more from a request for proposal/tender to evaluation and contract award. If you haven't seriously engaged with the prospect 180 days prior, your chances of winning are slim. Why? You need to establish influence and insights before the prospect hits the market, ensuring your brand and solution rank high in their decision process. While this isn't a fixed rule and some opportunities might take longer or shorter, it's a practical guide to timing.

Being familiar with your sales pipeline ratios necessary to hit your target is good practice for any professional. Here's an example:

Quarterly Target = $1,000,000

To achieve Target, I need:

A Close:Proposals submitted ratio of = 50%

So, I need to submit Proposals to the value of = $2,000,000 in opportunities

To achieve submitted Proposals of $2,000,000 I need:

A Meeting:Proposal submitted ratio of = 25%

So, I need to have Meetings to the value of = $8,000,000 in opportunities

To achieve having Meetings to the value of $8,000,000 I need:

A Prospecting:Meeting ratio of = 20%

So, I need to reach out to a Prospect patch value = $400,000,000

Once you know the size of the prospect patch needed to hit your target, you need to understand the results from previous activities and methods of approach. Remember, not all customers will be inclined to meet with you through one method. Understanding what works and what doesn't, through number evaluation, is extremely valuable. You can adjust, enhance, abandon, or multiply methods. Here's an example of success rates by prospecting type showing what percentage of meetings the Salesperson has secured from each activity:

Prospecting Type Success Breakdown

Calls to contacts : meetings ratio = 15%

Email : meeting ratio = 3%

Socials : meetings ratio = 5%

Network events : meetings ratio= 10%

Roundtable : meetings ratio = 25%

Referral leads : meetings ratio = 68%

Partner leads : meeting ratio = 70%

You'll observe some methods have high success rates and should be pursued zealously. Others might be lower but could be just as significant depending on the potential deal's value.

Here's a simple exercise:

Suppose you have a close ratio of 10% (1 in 10) and 20 opportunities in your pipeline. You sell to one of those 20. How many new opportunities do you need to add to your pipeline? If you answered 1, like I initially did, I'm afraid you're mistaken. The correct answer is 10 because you need 10 new opportunities to make one sale. Surprising, isn't it?

If you find yourself in a sales slump, instead of doubling down on the desperation to close, it's better to focus on building the pipeline for the next 90 to 180 days. Of course, you should pursue current opportunities, but not at the expense of pipeline growth, otherwise, you'll fall into a downward spiral of dwindling opportunities and rising excuses for unmet targets.

Never underestimate the importance of constantly building your sales pipeline. It needs to be a continuous flow for success and should be a part of your daily routine. Make sure you celebrate every new meeting and uncovered opportunity. You deserve it because you are turning nothing into something. Without your actions, the sales process stagnates, preventing any sales, revenue, or profit from flowing into the business. Embrace this mindset.

Sandra is an Account Director with a global tech company. She's 12 months into her role and facing pressure from her manager, whose weekly pipeline check-ins are highlighting a lack of opportunities to meet monthly sales targets. Sandra dreads these sessions. She attempts to emphasize the deals in the pipeline, but deep down, she knows they have less than a 25% chance of materializing.

For this week's review, she decides to be candid with her manager about the situation and seek help. Rather than scolding Sandra, her manager understands the predicament and together, they delve into the issue. They identify that Sandra is holding the right quota of meetings every week; however, she isn't translating these into a good ratio of proposals. They arrange for the manager to join Sandra in meetings that week, acting as an observer and coach.

After these meetings, the manager helps Sandra realize she is not delving deep enough into customer challenges, failing to uncover ways she can assist. They work on using customer testimonials and stories to make conversations more impactful. Three months later, Sandra's pipeline coverage to target has doubled from 2:1 to 4:1, bringing a corresponding increase in her sales. This reinforces the straightforward fact: "The more genuine opportunities you have, the more sales you make." Sandra no longer dreads the pipeline review sessions; she's confident in her numbers.

In this example, identifying the reasons for the lack of pipeline build was critical for success. Know your numbers and seek feedback from others. If you're open to advice, you will grow.

In summary:

- ➤ If you're struggling with inadequate sales opportunities or relying on a single deal to hit your: weekly, monthly, quarterly target, it's straightforward - you simply haven't created enough pipeline.
- ➤ Intense customer engagement needs to occur before they enter the market; otherwise, your chances are slim.
- ➤ Know your numbers. What pipeline creation $ do you need to achieve targets?
- ➤ When you win a sale, immediately replace the opportunity by the close ratio number. For example, if your close ratio is 10%, you need to create 10 new opportunities for each sale.
- ➤ Prospecting must become a daily habit. Ignoring it can be perilous.

PLAY 2.
SKILL UP TO WIN

WHAT QUESTIONS ARE IMPORTANT TO ASK AND HOW TO ASK THEM?

THE CLUE TO these important questions is in the words used. In his terrific book: 'Splitting the Difference', author Chris Voss, who is a former FBI hostage negotiator, explains brilliantly the power of calibrated questions. He demonstrates examples of how open questions from the negotiator, that gave the kidnappers a sense of control, empathy and understanding, saved hostages in life and death situations. Fortunately, as a Sales professional, you aren't faced with such strenuous circumstances. However, there are fantastic lessons from the techniques used.

Ok basics first. What is a closed question and what is an open question? A closed question is a question that can be answered in a factual way, or with a simple yes or no. EG:

- How many people work in your business? The answer will be short, just a number, perhaps they'll expand with commentary, but the question is closed.
- Do you want to buy a new car? - This elicits a yes or no answer.
- Did you see our advertisement on YouTube? - Again, it's a yes or no answer.

- When is your contract up? - The response can be a as short as a date.

An open question invites the other person to think, expand and articulate their answer. Listen to good interviewers and reporters on tv or your favourite podcast and you'll see some great examples. EG:

- How is your business managing staffing levels in this environment? - Notice this requires some thought from the responder and may provide some excellent business background to explore for opportunity.
- What would fulfilling that requirement mean for the business? - Here you are also tapping into a business benefit response.
- What is it about our proposal that you see as valuable?
- How will you look to improve the environment when your contract is up?

High gain open questions are more thought provoking for the customer. They take business questions to another level. EG:

- What will be the top 3 benefits to your customer base, when you implement solution x?
- How will the savings on capital expenditure effect your department over the next 12 months?
- If budget was endless, what would the dream solution look like?
- How would implementing this solution provide an advantage over competitors?

It's important to not fill the pause, the moments of silence between asking the question and the customer responding, by speaking. Observation is key. If the open question is one that you can see the customer is having to spend some moments thinking about, allow them the time. I've seen many a Salesperson's nervousness, or haste, get in the way, trying to put words into the customers mouth, by suggesting the answer. You can literally see the customer's eyebrows rise with an "Ok, we'll move on then" look.

Another consideration is being specific and efficient in your questions. Keep the question to one subject, with an answer that can only relate to that subject. The opposite of this is double barrelling. EG How will the HR and Sales team use the new laptop version? You can see that the customer here can answer generally for both departments. However, what will give you more insight and areas to assist with is asking the questions for each department. EG How will the HR team use the new laptop version? And following a discussion there, ask the same about Sales.

Each question type: closed or open, has its place. Closed questions will help build the story, get the needed facts required to build out your solution. However, you need to mine for the gold. You need to dig. Open questions, particularly 'How' and 'What', are the magic tools at your disposal to uncover the gold. These help you to: build rapport, show empathy, understanding and tailor your solution to the individual and business requirements.

How about asking a why question? Asking why, is a direct and powerful tool; however, it comes with some caveats, which I'll explain; but first, as an exercise for getting to the absolute bottom of anything, try doing the 5 why's technique. It goes like this:

Pick a topic to question and ask 5 why's to each answer.

1. EG: They say: "We need to reduce costs." You ask: "why?"

2. They answer: "It's a board directive." You ask: "why?

3. They answer:" It's been a tough year economically." You ask:" why?"

4. They answer:" It's a very competitive market." You ask: "why?"

5. They answer:" New low-cost suppliers are challenging us." You ask:" why?"

6. They answer: "Their international manufacturing costs are so low compared to ours."

What did you learn here? I reckon, a real nugget of understanding about a key challenge in their business: cost pressures from overseas competition. You wouldn't have known this without the drill down questioning. You could in fact keep drilling down.

I had some fun using this technique with my kids when they were young. I'd get them to do the 5 why's. It would go something like this:

1. I'd say: "People went to the moon." They'd say: "why?"

2. I'd say: "To explore space." They'd say: "why?"

3. I'd say: "To find out what's there." they'd say: "why?"

4. I'd say: "because it's exciting." They'd say: "why?"

5. I'd say: "because it's an adventure." they'd say: why?

6. I'd say: "because it's fun and amazing to discover new things." (A Nice education in helping create curious minds).

The challenge with the word or phrasing in using 'why', is it is very curt, short, direct, punchy and can come across as aggressive or challenging to the other person. Like "why would you do that? Why would you say that? Why would you think that? Think of a time someone challenged you with a direct why question. How did you feel? So, you do have to be careful with why questions? They need to be used with good intonation, that derives an inquisitive approach on the topic/subject, not in a way that's negatively questioning the person or organisations decisions.

Notice in this example below, how using 'what' as an alternative to why, de-risks any potential for the person to take an insult emotion from your question:

"Alan, you selected the service that is causing the issue; why?" Versus "Alan, what was it about the service causing the issue, that resulted in it being selected? "It's the same question, right? Just framed in a different way.

In your day-to-day life, be aware of how you are constructing these questions. See what reactions from people work/don't work. In Neil Rackham's book 'Spin Selling' he provides a framework for business sales questions. SPIN is an acronym for the type of questions that provide insights and value to the sale process.

- S is for 'situation' questions, the closed question type discussed earlier. EG: "How many staff do you have?"" How many computers do you have?"" Where are your offices located?" etc. These are necessary questions to uncover the basic inputs you'll require for your solution and proposal.

- P is for 'problem' questions. EG" What are the pain points?"" What are the issues?" These are the areas many salespeople will seek out and believe they have done a good job. A top sales professional will delve further, however.
- I is for 'implication' questions. EG: "what is the implication or impact for your team when that issue occurs?" This type of question draws out valuable insights on the specific impact for the person, team, or business. You are getting to the heart of the issue to address.
- N is for 'needs, pay off' IE: you ask a question that seeks their buy in to act on a need they have. EG" Mr customer, if an online report shows and alerts you to that cost blow out, will that be something you would implement?"

You can gauge the success of a discovery sales meeting by the number of 'Implication' and 'Needs, Pay Off' answers you have gathered. It shows a deep understanding of their specific challenges and what they will act on to address those challenges. A top salesperson will capture these and present compelling answers for the customer in their executive summary proposal.

Mark is Procurement Manager for a large state-based utility company. He receives two proposals for the supply of office products. One of the proposals is an obvious templated response showcasing the sellers' products, services, prices and how great they are as a company. It's high level with no demonstration in knowledge of the customers business and challenges to resolve. It's generic.

The other proposal lays out a clear understanding of the key challenges from their current provider, the impact on end users, and commercial impact to the business. It also demonstrates the key initiatives that the utility company see as important to address, and how they will specifically apply their solution and the resulting benefits in commercial savings and efficiency gains.

What's the difference between these two proposals? Well one clearly shows that the Salesperson has asked detailed questions to understand the utility companies' challenges and needs from Company level to individual level. It gives Mark in his procurement role, confidence in the Salesperson and his Company. They are showing that they understand Mark's business and demonstrating how exactly they will support them. Mark's choice in selection has been made a lot easier for him.

In summary:

> Be mindful of the types of questions to ask to get a great outcome.

> Master 'how and what' questions to drill down and understand with detail customers situations and emotions.

- ➢ Ask high value questions, that are thought provoking for the customer.
- ➢ Remember to not fill the silence after asking a question.
- ➢ Avoid double barrelling questions. Be specific in subject to avoid generalisation answers.
- ➢ Why questions can be too direct and taken poorly, so watch your phrasing/tone/intonation.
- ➢ Identify the type of information you are receiving from the customer. Is it factual, an issue or problem for the customer, a need, something they will act against.

ACTIVE LISTENING

HAVE YOU EVER encountered a Salesperson who seemed to speak incessantly, as if in a race against time, spewing out their sales pitch without respite? It feels as though they are racing against the countdown clock of an impending catastrophe, akin to a scene in a James Bond film, urgently blurting out their message before time runs out.

I vividly remember a multimillion-dollar contract proposal presentation I attended. The company had spent months meticulously collecting information for a consultative solution, and now was the moment to present it to the client. An internal preparation meeting was held, a plan was agreed upon, and various expert speakers were assigned portions of the presentation. The Business Development Manager (BDM) was charged with introducing the agenda and transitioning to the team. However, in the customer's boardroom, the BDM began to speak and seemed to forget to pause for breath. In a breathless 10–15-minute soliloquy, he unleashed every detail of the upcoming presentation and solution, drowning the clients in an avalanche of information. Within minutes, you could see the clients' attention waning, their focus wandering as they were inundated by the relentless wave of words.

At the esteemed Harvard negotiation school, students learn the art of balancing empathy and assertion: assertion allows you to explain your viewpoint, and empathy lets you see the world through the other person's eyes. The BDM needed this balance; he needed to present his information concisely while recognizing and responding to the customers' verbal and nonverbal cues.

This process necessitates full presence and attentiveness, to:

a. Listen carefully to the other person's narrative and messaging.

a. Observe their body language.

a. Decode these inputs while preparing your own verbal and body language responses.

Active listening is a challenging skill to master. The human mind is easily distracted, wandering off to ponder other matters such as emails, reports, or personal concerns. This tendency of our minds to flit from one thought to another like monkeys in a tree is referred to as 'The Monkey Mind' in Buddhism. To practice active listening, you must concentrate, focusing on the client's narrative, seeking to understand it, and if you don't, requesting clarification. This demonstrates your desire to understand their story.

Brain coach Jim Kwik suggests an easy-to-remember acronym for enhancing attention and memory: MOM.

- M represents Motivation. You must have a strong reason to listen and remember. Why is this information important to you?

- O stands for Observation. You must actively observe the other person's body language, words, phrasing, and intonation.
- M refers to Mechanics. These are the techniques you can use to improve memory and manage and train your recall.

As Kwik says, "It's not about retention, it's about attention."

Being truly present with people, giving them your undivided attention and listening fully rather than preparing your next statement, is potent. The word listen also spells silent – a worthwhile reminder.

Mastering active listening will ensure your success in both short-term and long-term sales relationships. It will garner respect from others, a deep understanding of the customer's specific needs, and an effective way to convincingly communicate why your product/service/solution is an excellent match for them.

Patrick is a gregarious, extraverted, outgoing person who loves to chat and tell stories. He's the leading salesman in his city, successfully attracting new members to his company's loyalty program. Early in his career, Patrick's overbearing approach was off-putting for both his colleagues and customers, leaving them feeling overwhelmed by his nonstop monologue.

Fortuitously, Patrick was receptive to feedback from a business Sales Coach hired by his company. Video role-plays of sales situations allowed Patrick to observe his tendency to dominate conversations and neglect active listening. With the coach's guidance, Patrick started to implement tactics such as waiting for the speaker to finish their statement before responding, reflecting back what the speaker had just said, and consciously observing the customer's body language for communication signals. These subtle yet significant skills improved Patrick's results by an impressive 32% and shifted his colleagues' perception of him as a professional salesman.

In summary:

- ➤ Be attentive to the customer's words and body language. Absorb their feedback. Practice deep listening.
- ➤ Hone the skill to listen actively while formulating your responses.
- ➤ Strive to balance the expression of your message with empathizing with the customer's perspective.

NOTE TAKING

ACTIVE LISTENING, A pivotal trait for effective communication, is enhanced greatly by another vital skill: notetaking during meetings. You may hear salespeople declare, "I don't need to take notes; I can just remember it." This sentiment, however, merits scepticism. The research of memory pioneer Hermann Ebbinghaus, known as 'The forgetting curve', underscores that an average of 50% of information received is forgotten immediately, with 70% forgotten within 24 hours and 90% within a week.

Throughout my tenure in sales management, I've observed various approaches to note-taking during sales calls, training, or general meetings. Although salespeople aren't typically known for their administrative prowess, the notes you take form the blueprint for your response to the customer's unique challenges. Attempt to recall a conversation you had three to four weeks ago without referring to notes. Difficult, isn't it?

Review this post-sales-call coaching debrief, where the representative hasn't taken notes.

Coach: "How do you think the meeting went?"
Rep: "Really good. I see a fantastic opportunity."
Coach: "What aspects went well?"

Rep: "He's not satisfied with his current provider, and he's eager to save money. We can certainly help."

Coach: "Are there specific things we missed or could have improved for greater impact?"

Rep: "I can't think of anything."

Coach: "Did you manage to glean any significant business insights or strategies that are important to him?"

Rep: "Hmm..."

Coach: "I noted that their business is branching out into... Did you catch that?"

Rep: "Oh, yes, I remember now."

Coach: "What were the specific repercussions for the end users in their business due to the x challenge?"

Rep: "Hmm...they were losing money."

Coach: "I noted that they were 10% behind budget year to date and need to save 18% between now and June 30. Did you catch that?"

Rep: "Ah, yes, that's right."

At this juncture, the coach's confidence in the representative's ability to glean crucial insights from the customer conversation for a robust proposal is wavering. Without notes capturing key points, the rep is ill-equipped to deliver an A+ response. A lack of detail precludes them from adequately articulating or challenging the customer's needs and might earn them a mere C+. This is the difference between top-tier reps and their average counterparts.

So, which note-taking method works best? It comes down to personal preference, environment, and circumstance. Let's explore some options:

- **Note pad and pen:** Richard Branson, in his book 'Losing My Virginity,' professed his preference for this method, always carrying a small notebook to jot down ideas. A pen and paper feel more open and transparent during physical meetings than a laptop or tablet, which can serve as a barrier, obscuring information. A notepad on the table is visible to all and allows you to maintain eye contact while jotting down notes. Try making quick notes while keeping eye contact, remaining actively engaged in the conversation.

- **Laptop or tablet:** "Efficiency"—that's the magic of this method. Your notes from the meeting are digitized, captured once, and can be shared and referred to quickly if stored well. It's very common to enter a meeting where everyone has an open laptop, tapping away as someone is speaking, their eyes down and fingers furiously moving as they concentrate on the words hitting the screen. What you must be mindful of, however, is not losing the physical interaction of intently listening and observing the body language and communication style of the speaking customer. It's important to show them that you are actively interested and engaged with them. How? Well, simply through continual eye contact and perhaps mirroring what they have said to you to let them know you have understood.

- **Virtual meetings:** Notetaking during virtual meetings can be easily done on platforms like OneNote, Evernote, email, or Google Docs while maintaining visual contact with the other participants. Where someone is using pen and paper, you can visibly see the eyes move off camera to the side, but you can't see what they are writing, it's good to see that they are interested and taking notes, however it doesn't have the same impact as in a physical room.

- **Recording the meeting:** With technology allowing us to easily record on phones, laptops, and during virtual meetings, it's a great way to ensure absolute accuracy of the information gathered. This approach is commonplace in internal meetings such as training, brainstorming, and presentation sessions. It's also most useful for interviewing customers who are sharing their story as part of public relations exercises like case studies and media releases. In these examples, there is a comfort factor established through relationships and trust. For internal meetings, the information shared is in-house. For customers providing stories for joint PR, the messaging will be agreed upon and ratified by all parties before release.

So, what about in a sales setting, for example, a first call introduction? Well, it depends. What is the setting? If it's a one-on-one casual introduction, where you're attempting to build initial rapport, requesting to record may put up defences. The customer might think: "They want to record. Hmm, I need to be mindful of what I say." In this scenario, you achieve the opposite effect of what you want: defensiveness and a blunting of rapport building.

On the other hand, if it's a more formal setting such as a boardroom meeting with multiple team members from both parties present, requesting to record may be seen as very professional, diligent, efficient, and prudent. As it's a group setting, people will be very mindful of the information they're giving out anyway. The customer may think, "These guys really want to understand our business. All good."

Of course, the discipline for the salesperson then lies in listening to the recording or reading the automated text notes to capture the key points to address. Yes, that's right—you must put in additional time to review. It's easy to see the advantages if you do this well. You can concentrate fully on engagement during the meeting, without the need to take notes, and you can be accurate in the information gathered for any time in the future. A counterpoint to this is: if you are a good note-taker during a meeting, perhaps it's more efficient to simply capture those written/typed notes in the moment.

- **Storage of notes:** Digital notetaking offers the advantage of easy storage, tracking, and recalling of information. Whether you use a notes tool on your device or digital copies of your handwritten or recorded notes, they need to be easily accessible.

When we consider the reasoning behind notetaking, it becomes apparent that our brains, not engineered for retaining massive amounts of detail for instant recall, operate with a lean efficiency model. They store the essential, often emotionally tied, memories and keep the runway clear for immediate, surrounding inputs. Hence, notes must be accessible and ideally retrievable instantly. Digital storage is a clear winner in this regard. Let's illustrate this with a real-world example:

At 8:30 AM, Business Development Manager Joe sits in a café just a stone's throw away from his office. He gets a call from his Executive, who asks, "Joe, I'm seeing your client, ABC Ltd, in an hour. Anything specific I should be aware of?"

Joe's response is prompt: "Absolutely, let me pull up my latest notes. Just a moment."

He taps open his go-to note application on his smartphone, types in 'ABC Ltd' in the search bar, and there they are—his notes from a meeting two months ago. "Alright, we're in business. The client is involved in....."

As long as the notetaking is clear and consistent, and ideally consolidated in one place for easy reference, this system's efficiency is extraordinary. Handwritten notes are no exception—even a scan or a digital photograph of the page works wonders, allowing you to digitize and store without having to type it all up again.

In summary:

> ➢ No matter the method, ensure you note down crucial details. The client will perceive you as professional, attentive, and committed to remembering the conversation.
> ➢ Maintain eye contact. Cultivate the skill of writing/typing with minimal distraction from the customer.
> ➢ Consider the environment and the context of your meeting. Could recording the meeting yield advantages?
> ➢ Your capacity to remember the discussed points in the days, weeks, or even years ahead will elevate you above the average performer.

PROPOSAL WRITING AND THE EXECUTIVE SUMMARY

"YOU CAN TELL the quality of the Salesperson by the quality of the Executive summary in the proposal."

In the realm of business sales, an executive summary must be of such calibre that a customer would feel confident presenting it to their top-level executives. This succinct encapsulation of your proposed solution for their business issues is pivotal. But what should such a summary comprise? As always in sales, consider the perspective of the customer—what would they want to see?

Here are some key elements to include:

- A succinct display of your understanding of their business direction. A couple of insightful paragraphs about their strategic goals—be they revenue growth, efficiency gains, cost reduction, or customer service—can achieve this.
- Clearly demonstrate how the strategic business direction stands to benefit from the proposed improvements or actions. Highlight why they should review this particular challenge.
- Concisely list the issues they are grappling with and the specific impact these have on their business. This is where

the salesperson's skill in eliciting insights from the customer comes to the fore. The proposal must articulate the exact pain points and their implications: lost productivity, efficiency, time, revenue, and so forth. If you can quantify this in monetary terms—either losses or gains—even better.

- Cost Highlight. Many proposals relegate pricing to the back of the document. However, in a meeting, customers invariably flip to the final pages to scan the cost. If you're outside of their budget range, they'll tune out, regardless of your beautifully crafted pitch. There should be no surprises here—the best salespeople will have already established the budget range before the proposal is written. The cost or value proposition should be introduced early in the summary, right after the issues and challenges. A headline like **"$1,264,567 Cost Savings"** is a powerful motivator—the executives will be thinking, "this merits further attention."
- Provide a summary table comparing past and new figures. Detailed analysis can be reserved for the main body of the proposal.
- Summarize, in bullet form, how your solution addresses the identified business challenges.
- Include a section on your company's credibility—referrals, history, accreditations, strengths.

By encapsulating these elements within the executive summary, the main comprehensive proposal can delve into further detail.

Most organizations use templates for specific products or solutions, but these should be customized for each client.

PowerPoint Proposals

Choosing between a written proposal and a PowerPoint presentation depends on several factors, such as the audience and the environment. If you're presenting to a group, PowerPoint is generally better as it allows you to control the flow and pace of the message.

When using PowerPoint, it should reflect the key points in the executive summary. Continually check in with the customer to ensure understanding and agreement. Confirmation questions like "does that make sense?" or "have we got that right?" are useful. It's far better to get feedback during the presentation than leaving unsure of your standing.

Anita is among the top three sales professionals nationally, standing out among her 63 colleagues. She represents a fleet vehicle servicing business.

Janet, an external sales trainer, is engaged by the company to assess the team and determine the best strategies for improving performance. The assessment includes reviewing recently submitted proposals to prospective customers. She discovers that Anita's proposal style is customer-centric, particularly evident in the Executive Summary. Anita demonstrates an understanding of the customers' specific challenges and their impact on departmental and individual efficiency. Utilizing the customers' own naming conventions and language in her descriptions, she ensures relevance and impact. Anita clearly highlights the potential savings for the customer early in the Executive Summary and succinctly outlines how her company will cater to the business. Notably, Anita provides the customers with a hard-copy document as well as a corresponding PowerPoint presentation used during the decision committee meeting. An excellent strategy!

In contrast, the lower-performing salespeople submit generic, templated proposals with little to no personalization, merely changing the name. In some instances, Janet even finds other customers' names in proposals, evidence of careless copying and pasting. Additionally, she observes a low level of note-taking and calibrated questioning during customer visits by these underperforming representatives.

It's clear to Janet why Anita consistently outperforms her peers. Her recommendation to management is to use Anita's work as a benchmark in coaching sessions, enabling local managers to guide sales representatives in the field. By setting a higher standard of quality, the team's overall results will likely improve.

In summary:

- ➢ Demonstrate your knowledge of their business strategy in relation to the challenges/needs in the Executive Summary.
- ➢ Show how the challenges and issues will impact their business in detail.
- ➢ Provide a headline commercial benefit early in the Executive Summary. Don't hide it at the end of the proposal.
- ➢ Explain why they should select your business with compelling credibility statements in the Executive Summary.
- ➢ Be comprehensive in your proposal document.

➢ Mirror the Executive Summary in your PowerPoint presentation.
➢ Seek immediate feedback and guidance from the customer during the presentation.

OBJECTIONS, CONTRACT NEGOTIATIONS AND EXECUTION

"YES, WE'VE WON, we got the deal!" shouts out the excited Sales Rep."

Celebrations reverberate throughout the office. A call from the client has affirmed their choice to offer the major contract. Premature congratulations, high fives, and pats on the back fill the air. Fast forward six weeks, the same client rescinds their offer, citing a change in direction. A deal isn't sealed until the agreement is approved, ratified, and signed, whether digitally or in ink.

This is a career-defining lesson that many salespeople encounter. A verbal approval may falter during final diligence, in the face of a counteroffer, with a change in personnel, or any number of reasons a client might have to renege on the agreement. It's the elusive, a deal isn't done until the signature is on the contract – a tough pill to swallow, especially after announcing a major victory to colleagues. So, apart from refraining from premature celebrations, how should a salesperson navigate this phase of the deal?

Primarily, stay calm and understand that objections, whether valid or otherwise, are integral to the sales process until the final sign-off. This is where you truly prove your mettle. Do you possess the skills to decipher the real reasons for their sudden change of heart?

"No" might simply be a request for more information, a need for more convincing reasons to choose your solution.

Positioning how your solution provides enhanced value over the competitors is an art. Everyone will be pitching their solution as the best. Approach with the knowledge of what you know for sure. Use public consultancy reviews, whitepapers, videos, customer voices with real experience of the competition. Show the customer that you know what they are considering. You have that intelligence. Check in with them if you are missing anything. Once you have done this - present the reality of how you add compelling value over and above the competitor(s). Ideally this objection handling is pre-empted in your proposal stage. However, a customer may have overlooked it, forgotten it in the myriad of information, or simply seen your solution as less value. If you are on the wrong end of the decision, you will have to address.

Consider a time you were about to make a significant purchase or investment – a house, a car, a vacation – and found yourself changing your mind. An influential conversation, a compelling piece of information, something shifted your perspective enough to alter your course. Just like Indiana Jones selecting the safe path across a perilous chasm, a skilled salesperson identifies the stepping stones – pieces of tailored information – that will help the customer achieve their goals and choose your solution over the competition.

At this stage, patience, understanding, and professional assertiveness are crucial. Clients need reassurance that they've made the correct decision for their business. It's your responsibility to provide this reassurance and guide them through the contract approval process.

Nowadays, most contracts are approved digitally and shared via email, deviating from traditional face-to-face negotiations. This shift can eliminate the age-old tactics of reading body language and asking, "your pen or mine?" However, it indicates that the negotiations have made the buyer confident in their decision, based on the merit of the solution, not a persuasive sales technique.

A digital signature is not equivalent to a face-to-face meeting. There's something to be said about the handshake, the eye contact, the unspoken transfer of trust. Always aim to set up a contract sign-off meeting, even if the customer insists, they'll sign digitally. At least you've made the attempt.

I've participated in captivating final negotiations where customers minutely review every aspect of the deal, contract, all with pen patiently in hand. While it's evident that the contract will be signed, a degree of patience, active listening, and addressing all remaining queries is essential to assure the customer. The customer inevitably says, "Ok, let's finalize this," and signs the agreement. This step is driven by the customer without any hard-sell closing techniques. You've reached an agreement, and the customer signs because they see the mutual benefit. It's an ideal way to kickstart a partnership with your client.

Sienna, the lead sales rep, receives a call from the CIO of a major global education provider. Her bid for new accounting software has been accepted. The win is a massive victory for her, ensuring she meets her annual sales target. Although the news fills her with joy, she maintains her composure, acknowledging the work that lies ahead. She expresses gratitude to the client for the opportunity and outlines the contract approval steps. She also confirms if they need any additional assistance. They agree on a plan for the coming week for the client to review the contract and its terms. Sienna offers a meeting with their legal counsel if needed, to address any potential queries from the client's contract team.

A week later, Sienna touches base with the CIO to check on the progress. The CIO informs her that their lawyer has some concerns about the terms. Sienna doesn't let panic set in. She suggests their lawyer highlight the problematic clauses and send them over. She will arrange a meeting between their team and hers. The CIO concurs.

The following day, the client's objections arrive. Sienna discusses these with her legal team. They accept some changes, but any further amendments require approval from the Managing Director. Sienna shares this with the client's CIO. She proposes that, given the need for higher-level approval, their Managing Director should also attend the meeting. The CIO agrees – the investment is substantial and requires Board approval.

Sienna coordinates a meeting in the client's boardroom, including her legal counsel and Managing Director. She also organizes a preparation meeting two days prior to explain what's needed. She confirms with the client's CIO that everything is in order and their Managing Director can attend. The meeting is set.

On the day of the meeting, Sienna orders coffee for everyone, knowing the value of breaking bread. She thanks everyone for their presence, acknowledges the opportunity, and recounts the journey leading to this point. She then lets the legal counsel discuss the disputed clauses. With the help of both Managing Directors, they agree on a compromise and a revised contract is to be prepared within 24 hours for approval. Sienna thanks everyone for their time and effort. She schedules a follow-up meeting with the CIO in two days to sign off on the agreement, allowing a 24-hour window for them to review the final terms.

Sienna ensures the agreement is sent to the client for final review the next day. The CIO responds an hour later, stating they won't be able to sign the following day because their Managing Director received a call from the current provider. At this point, Sienna feels her heart sink. She understands, however, that this is just another obstacle to overcome. She remains composed and enquires about the nature of the discussion. The CIO replies, "Well, they've demanded a meeting and he's known them for a while, so he's going to hear them out. If there is any problem, I'll let you know."

Quickly, Sienna drafts a bulleted summary highlighting the reasons for leaving the incumbent provider, and how their solution will improve the client's service and profitability. The CIO appreciates the effort.

Despite being on tenterhooks, Sienna waits patiently. She's worked on this deal for a year and is so close to sealing it. In the afternoon, after the MD's meeting with the incumbent, she calls the CIO. He reassures her, "It's all good, Sienna. I've received the go-ahead to sign your contract. I'll complete that tomorrow morning." This time, Sienna can barely contain her joy. Maintaining her composure, she suggests, "That's fantastic news. How about I join you tomorrow morning, and we can sign off together?" The CIO agrees.

The next day, Sienna walks into the office with a signed contract in hand. Now, it's time to ring the bell.

Sales stories can be like mini movies. They have heroes, villains, wise characters who guide, a mountain climb, with an inevitable drama or curveball that knocks you off track, only for the protagonist to pick themselves up, and carry on, removing the boulders put in their way, and finally with the help of their band of cohorts, win the day!

In this narrative, Sienna embodies professionalism. She remains cool and collected, facilitating each stage, knowing that the deal isn't done until it's done.

In summary:

> ➢ Relax. Do not let the thrill of nearing the finish line distract you. Remember, you are not over the line yet.
> ➢ Determine the essential objection steppingstones that need addressing. Ask calibrated questions to engage the client, guiding them with more tailored information to establish the superiority of your solution.
> ➢ Identify what's required for approval and list the actions needed. These could include providing your contract and

terms for review, providing references, aligning your Executive and legal counsel with theirs.

➤ Take charge of these steps. Supply the client promptly with all relevant documents and resources. Manage your internal resources to meet the client's timeline. You are the conductor of the orchestra; a single off-note could jeopardize the deal.

➤ Schedule meetings with the client and set a target sign-off date. This gives everyone a clear goal to work towards.

➤ Attempt to be present for the sign-off with the client. A handshake can be a powerful symbol of a new partnership built on trust.

➤ Stay engaged post sign-off. Take responsibility.

THE 12 STEPS IN THE SALES CYCLE

AWARENESS OF THE sales cycle and one's current position within it is imperative. Throughout this process, you'll juggle multiple targets and opportunities. It's tempting to skim over each stage, thinking, "I'm proficient, there's no need to delve deeper, I'm too occupied." However, skimming might result in lost deals. It's undeniable that more could have been done. To maintain a place among the top 20% of performers, follow these steps with thoroughness and adopt an in-depth approach.

1. **Begin by identifying your Target Market.** Determine who could be potential customers. Numerous consultancy and media firms have detailed information about businesses in your geographic area. You don't need to reinvent the wheel. Invest in information about these companies: their industry, employee count, location, and recent financials. This information will help identify businesses that align well with your product or service.

Your market size could include 10,000 companies to approach, or perhaps only 200. Regardless of the size, it's crucial to identify your target. Picture a helicopter flying out at sea, where an ocean of disaster awaits a careless landing. It's far better to concentrate on locating a safe ship to land on. Better yet, envision a brightly painted circle with a big 'H' in the middle, clearly marked on the ship. That's the level of focus required in sales. So, what does the 'H' represent in sales? It's a specifically curated list of companies that fit certain criteria, companies you know will respond positively to what you're selling. Retargeting the Market every 6 to 12 months, depending on your industry, is strongly advised. Stay aware of the ever-shifting market and the companies that offer the best opportunities.

2. **Review your existing customers.** Understand their demographics, challenges, reasons for choosing you, and previous suppliers. Essentially, you're identifying the attributes that drive customers to your business. This knowledge can then be applied to your prospect list.

Once you've gleaned insights from your existing customers, overlay this lens onto your prospect list and narrow it down further. If the overall market size is 10,000, how do you whittle that down to 500, 100, or even the top 10 targets? You may consider factors like size of spend, number of employees, industry type, geography, known contract end dates, or business changes. Add concentric target rings to your helipad metaphor with the 'H' bullseye in the middle. Develop a marketing plan tailored to these targets.

3. **Conduct in-depth company research.** This includes online research, social media perusal, and consulting contacts for insights. Develop an understanding of their organizational structure, key influencers, and decision makers. Recognize how their annual business initiatives might influence your

interactions with them. Even if you feel your solution sells itself, taking the time to understand your prospects can make a huge difference in long-term success.

4. **Initiate communication that connects** with their business needs. Ask yourself, what aspects of your phone call, email, LinkedIn message, or event invitation will capture their interest? A proven tactic is to employ a compelling story or example about how an organization or individual, similar to your target, has benefited from your services. The more intimate your knowledge of their business, the sharper your focus will be. The specificity of your headline could make all the difference. For instance, you might highlight a financial benefit like, 'Customer X reduced operational costs by 20% by adopting Solution Y over the past year' or 'Customer X boosted sales revenue by 7% eighteen months after implementing our solution.'

Existing customer testimonials and case studies, particularly those that narrate the journey from challenges to triumphs achieved through your solution, are invaluable assets. They illustrate tangible benefits like cost savings, improved customer service, or enhanced operational efficiency. An effective marketing team is key to breathing life into these narratives. While your ability to articulate these success stories is crucial, having written resources to supplement your pitch adds substantial value.

When it comes to events, consider what topics or guest speakers would entice your audience. Possible subjects could range from industry insights to broader themes impacting various sectors, such as cybersecurity, economic pressures, climate change, or customer service. Remember, the theme must resonate with your audience on a personal level to motivate them to participate.

5. **1st Meeting** - Prepare for the first meeting with knowledge of their business and how your solution fits. Use both closed and open questions to understand their world and needs.

6. **2nd + Meetings** - In subsequent meetings, involve your specialists to build understanding and demonstrate how your offering fits their needs.

7. **Proposal Readiness and Presentations** - Remember, if you've done a stellar job up to this point, your proposal should simply articulate what they have already indicated they need and are willing to accept. The quality of your proposal and executive summary will reflect the effectiveness of your sales process.

8. **Contractual/Legal Negotiations** - Depending on the complexity of the sale, both parties may need to further negotiate terms and conditions to reach a level that is acceptable for all involved.

9. **Once a contract is signed, seamlessly transition** to the project and delivery team.

10. **Post-Sale Support** - This is an essential component in cultivating robust customer relationships. Stay engaged to ensure alignment between your team and the customer, fulfilling the promises made during the sale and outlined in the contract. Some salespeople, unfortunately, earn a reputation akin to 'shark salesmen' - charming until the contract is signed, only

to vanish without a trace or fail to return customer calls and messages, passing off responsibilities with statements like "That's someone else's job; reach out to them." This is a damaging image, not just for the individual, but for the business as a whole. Such practices are typically unearthed, making it difficult for these individuals to sustain a high-performing sales career. It's more rewarding - professionally and personally - to invest time in genuinely caring about the people you interact with, be they customers or colleagues.

11. **Celebrate project completion with the customer.** Depending on the scale, this could be a shared meal or drinks.

12. **Customer References and Testimonials** - When you and your team excel in the sales and delivery process, customers will enthusiastically share their positive experiences. This aspect is vital and adroitly exploited by top-performing salespeople. Why? It not only showcases the customer's wise choices and impressive work but also amplifies the credibility of your narrative. The more customers Voice their excellent experiences with your business, the more you amplify your sales potential.

Bestselling author James Allen (Bain & Company) describes the idea of the 'Perfect Analogy'. It's where the skill of the salesperson identifies the unique requirements of the customer, matching them through storytelling to a previous customer experience. The more the story specifically relates to the customers purchase criteria, the higher the value in the story. Think of a time recently when you were making a large purchase; I expect friends or colleagues' stories of their experience for the same purchase helped you feel more assured in your decision. That is what you are looking for with your customer.

General testimonial use is ok, it helps with credibility, however it is the arena of average salespeople. Think above that level for maximum results.

PLAY 3.
COLLABORATE FOR SUCCESS

TEAM SELLING

IN A RETAIL environment, the art of selling tends to be individual-focused, contrasting the business-to-business corporate sales model. A customer enters the store, browses, or goes directly to their item of choice. Ideally, the salesperson engages with an open-ended question regarding what they're seeking, offers suggestions, provides product information, and completes the sale promptly at the checkout.

Contrastingly, in business sales, the buyer represents a group — their company — rather than making individual purchases. They are accountable for their decisions and are evaluated by their colleagues and superiors. The majority of business transactions involve a decision-making group that assesses predefined criteria. Depending on the purchasing department or area, this group may include Procurement Managers, Finance Managers, Department Managers, Specialists, Risk Managers, Operations Managers, HR Managers, Legal Counsel, C-level Executives, and Board members, among others. Satisfying such a diverse group from multiple disciplines on your own to persuade them that your solution is superior is an imposing challenge.

This situation necessitates a team approach, aligning the skills and attributes of your team to match those of the customer's. Wisely charting out the customer's organizational structure in relation to influencers and decision-makers relevant to your discussions is an effective strategy. As a salesperson in this scenario, you function as the orchestra conductor: setting up meetings for the right people, ensuring effective messaging, aligning communications, and orchestrating all parties towards a common goal. If, as an orchestra conductor, you permit the violins to play too softly, the brass too loudly, or the percussion out of rhythm, the music will sound discordant, and the listener will disengage. The same applies to business sales — as the conductor of the process, your role is to maintain harmony for optimal performance.

The early steps in a corporate sale will usually be your responsibility as the salesperson, starting with an initial discovery or introduction meeting. It's beneficial to be as informed as possible about the subject and the customer's environment. A colleague of mine shared how he conducted over 30 meetings with individual stakeholders of a major national supermarket chain to gain the best insights to share with his team and the supermarket's senior management. Against all odds, he and his team won that multimillion-dollar pursuit, despite facing a formidable incumbent.

But remember, you don't need to be the subject matter expert or specialist. Your strength lies in opening the door and fostering a two-way channel between the businesses. Initially, your goal is merely to generate enough interest to advance to a further meeting, where a more in-depth discovery session can take place with your solution experts and their key personnel. Your role then involves leveraging the insights of your team and the customer's guidance, ensuring that you're on track throughout the sales process. As the conductor, it's your job to keep everything in tune, on pitch, and on track.

The team dynamic encourages the sharing of ideas, skills, motivation, and challenges, all of which provide enhanced insights for the customer to consider. It's invaluable during customer meetings to be able to read the room, collect your thoughts, and prepare insightful questions or statements while a team member is speaking.

And let's not forget the joy of celebrating a win as a team. Who doesn't appreciate that!

Malcolm is the Chief Procurement Manager of a large healthcare charity organization. Tasked with tendering for power and electricity supply for their national premises, he and his managerial committee of six people from various roles in the business shortlist three bidders.

Two are satisfactory, capable of meeting the requirements for the bid. Yet, one stands out. Their bidding team, led by a persuasive salesperson, introduces experts in technical, financial, operational, and delivery roles. They explain how their solution meets the requirements and provide proven examples of recent experiences with customers. Each of Malcolm's decision committee members have their individual queries answered confidently and professionally. Despite the inherent uncertainty of all new contracts, the winning team puts them at ease with their compelling bid.

In this instance, the salesperson did an outstanding job of identifying the required team to align with the customer's committee members and understanding exactly what those members required.

If the salesperson had gone it alone, or with inappropriate support, the outcome would have been different.

In summary:

> Be knowledgeable and remember your role as a facilitator.
> Don't attempt to be a Lone Ranger – engage team specialists.
> Map out the customer's influencers and stakeholders relative to your sale.
> Open the door and align your team.
> Be the conductor of both the customer and your team - keep everything on pitch.
> Celebrate your victories as a team.

HOW TO LEVERAGE SALES MANAGERS TO WIN

THE WEEKLY SALES forecast call is upon you, and your Manager poses that cliff-hanger question: "So, what's your sales number going to be this week/month/quarter?" Depending on your recent performance and the prospects in your sales pipeline, this can either be your moment to shine or a moment of stress. If it's the former, you relish sharing the glowing details of upcoming sales, the strategic moves that led you there, and the excitement over pending deals. You exude confidence; life is good. However, if it's the latter and your sales funnel looks sparse, salespeople often resort to various tactics. You might overstate the potential of deals with slim chances, or resort to laying blame on external factors like market competition or indecisive customers.

So, what's the issue here? This may seem like typical sales funnel conversation, but the core problem is a lack of collaboration, a team-based approach, and perhaps even trust, all clouded by an underlying fear of failure. Sales, in the business context, are black and white: there's a target to meet. Any shortfall not only impacts your earnings but potentially puts your job at risk. Consistently covering up poor performance forecasts misses the opportunity to build a trusting relationship with your manager, which should be mutually beneficial.

Let's shift our gaze to your Sales Manager's perspective. Understanding what success means for those who gauge your performance is vital. If they succeed through you, you become invaluable—a win-win scenario.

Managers have targets. Being aware of these and showing concern for how your performance influences theirs positions you as a team player. Asking questions like, "What does the team need to achieve this month?" or "How can I make a difference this quarter?" can offer you a wider view and fuel your drive to meet your own sales targets.

Managers also must submit their own forecasts to higher-ups. Accurate reporting aids in organizational planning across operations, delivery, and finances. This chain of reporting reaches the top echelons, informing decisions that impact the entire company. Recognizing this big picture underlines the need for accuracy in your own forecasting.

So, how can you optimize your relationship with your Sales Manager to clinch wins? A good Manager aims to pave the way for your success. They can:

1. Clear internal roadblocks that impede progress toward a deal.

2. Provide support during customer interactions, adding depth to the conversation.

3. Facilitate peer-to-peer engagements to build multi-level relationships with customers.

4. Challenge you to stretch your capabilities further.

5. Coach you by observing and guiding your actions, using frameworks like ASGIW or GROW.

Here are examples of the Coach/Manager conversations using these frameworks:

ASGIW:

A - Accomplish - What is it in the sales call/meeting that you specifically wanted to accomplish? How did you go with achieving that goal?

S - Strengths - What were your strengths towards that goal. What did you do well?

G - Gaps - What gaps did you have towards the goal. What aspects could you improve?

I - Impact - What one or two things could you do differently or work on that would have most impact on achieving the goal next time?

W - What next - What will you do next as an action to improve?

GROW:

G - What is the goal you want to achieve? Be specific.

R - Realistic - Is it something that you can realistically achieve at a stretch.

O - Options – Ok park that goal. What are other options you can look at?

W - What next - What are the specific actions you will take towards the chosen goal?

Don't hesitate to engage openly with your manager, whether things are going well or not. The onus is on you to meet both your personal and business objectives. Yet, to excel, you must efficiently collaborate with your support team.

Anthony was worried. Two quarters of low-volume software sales were not only hitting his bank account but also looking bad on the national sales ladder chart. There were a couple of long shot deals to be worked on, but they were very much best-case scenarios. He wasn't looking forward to this morning's forecast call with his manager, Cathy. Cathy was tough on numbers, no excuses. The meeting started. Two of Anthony's colleagues, who were performing exceptionally, shared their pipeline-to-close numbers with details of specific deals for the upcoming quarter. "Brilliant, great work guys, you're on track to overachieve; keep up the good work," Cathy said. "Now, Anthony, what have you got in play to close the gap for the year?" All eyes turned to Anthony. "Well, Cathy, it's looking great," he said. "I will be closing out customers A and B next month, which will get me above target. We have made excellent progress, and the procurement managers are highly engaged in both accounts." Cathy dug a bit deeper: "What does their financial stakeholder say they like about our offer, as we know they'll be making the final call?" Anthony hesitatingly stated, "Ah, yes, they're good." "Great, well, if you need any help, let me know," Cathy replied. Anthony had fallen into the trap of pitching a positive story based on the hope of a turnaround in fortune.

Two months later, Anthony met with Cathy. Neither of the expected sales had materialized. Anthony's sales ratio hadn't improved. Worse yet, the failure to secure the deals meant the business had fallen short of the expected targets for the year. That meant Cathy had underachieved too. "Anthony, two months ago you said you would close out customer A and B sales. You said the finance approver was good with us, and no help was required when I asked. With both opportunities lost, what's your explanation?"

This is the awkward conversation that should never have to happen. If Anthony had been upfront in the forecast meeting, explaining exactly where each deal was positioned, and asking for assistance from Cathy and the business, he would have given himself the best chance of getting support from Cathy and the broader team. Any gaps in strategy and meeting customer requirements would have been challenged by the team and addressed. At worst, the gap in sales numbers would have been called out early, so Cathy, as manager, could report up concerns and request further business help. By not being upfront and accurate, how would you assess Cathy's trust in Anthony as a team performer? Not good, right?

In summary:

> Strategize with your Sales Manager for key pursuits.
> Ask for help to navigate internal business hurdles.
> Solicit coaching using frameworks like ASGIW or GROW.

- Involve them in customer meetings for added depth.
- Use peer-to-peer engagements to build wider relationships.
- Maintain transparency regarding your sales pipeline.

IT'S ALL ABOUT THE PRODUCT, RIGHT?

"WE OFTEN HEAR, 'The right product sells itself.' This sentiment usually comes from disheartened salespeople grappling with unmet targets or the aftermath of a key deal loss. But does the product truly sell itself?

Take for instance, marquee brands like iPhone, PlayStation, Coca Cola, McDonalds, Gucci, BMW, and countless others. Yes, people will eagerly queue overnight for an iPhone, pre-order the latest PlayStation months ahead, or go out of their way for McDonalds. However, all these brands have competitors, detractors, and opposition from sales and marketing teams.

'But isn't it easier to sell the best product?' This question is subjective, as the 'best' product or service can vary from one person to the next. It's the salesperson's skill that makes the difference - understanding the customer's unique needs and values, their specific problems and opportunities. Indeed, you need an excellent product or service that fulfills a market need and delivers on its promises. If it doesn't, consider seeking a more competitive business to represent. Yet, resist falling into the trap of blaming the product, your geographical area, or any other excuse for lack of success.

Challenge this mindset by examining your sales team's high achievers. How did they score their wins? Arrange a coffee date or a phone call to dive into their strategies. Emulate their successful behaviours, skills, and knowledge to up your game. Avoid being swayed by naysayers peddling discouraging words that only feed your excuses.

Scott has recently joined a corporate entertainment business, a rising star in the industry with some significant victories against the three major players in the field.

As part of his first two-week orientation, he observes several sales calls with the sales team. He listens to conversations both in the office and on the road, gaining insight into team dynamics. He takes note of a clique within the team, echoing sentiments like "we need more marketing," "the big guys are too embedded in the account," and "we need more testimonials."

Wisely, Scott seeks out those who've recently clinched contracts, requesting sessions to understand their winning strategies. In these sessions, he learns that they determined early on whether there was an appetite for change among their customers—i.e., whether there was a reason, cause, or motivation to change if the solution was right. Simply because customers were affiliated with large, established providers, it didn't guarantee their unwavering loyalty. Scott found that these customers highly valued certain aspects of service: competitiveness, agility, personalization, and flexibility. These qualities effectively competed against the more bureaucratic, less dynamic incumbents.

A Wall Street Executive barked to our seated and huddled head office team, as he paced at the head of the large meeting room. "You guys in marketing and support are the ground crew, the air traffic controllers, the refuelers. You're on the ground, low in personal risk but vital to the battle. Sales are the jet pilots, dog fighting up there in the sky. When you win, you are the heroes, you get the confetti. But when you lose, you crash and burn fast."

It was the 90's, and like a scene from the famous movie Glengarry Glen Ross with Alec Baldwin or Wolf of Wall Street with Leonardo di Caprio, the top city HQ Executive has come in, letting people know exactly where they stand. His messaging stayed with me. Without marketing and sales support teams (the guys on the ground), the chances of success for the Salesperson (the pilot) are slim. You could be the 'Top Gun' of sales but if you want to keep flying, you need that support crew, behind you, keeping you flying.

So how do you leverage the marketing side? How do you get the best out of your business resources? You must think of yourself as your own business, your own marketer, responsible for your own patch, your own results. The key areas to focus on include:

1. Understand your target customers. Categorize them by industry, size, fit to your solutions, and other relevant criteria.

2. Obtain contact details through direct outreach or tools like LinkedIn, AI.

3. Engage with the marketing team. Understand their plans, campaigns, and events, and align these with your communications to your target lists.

4. Plan your campaigns and use your marketing team's resources to ensure professional presentation.

5. Organize customer events, leveraging marketing for assistance with invitations, venues, and ideas. You drive it.

6. Collaborate with Marketing to create and publish compelling testimonials.

We often hear sales teams demanding more marketing, but taking initiative can significantly boost your results. Remember, if marketing was 100% successful, there'd be no need for salespeople. In business, the people-to-people connections, assurances, and relationships that salespeople nurture are vital to the buying process.

Francesca has shot to the top of the sales ladder competition over the course of the year. The corporate travel business she operates in has announced that she has won "around the world trip" tickets for her efforts. The sales team is asking how someone who was in the middle of the field the year before came through so strong. The marketing guys know how, though.

Francesca was meeting them weekly, letting them know what she specifically needed to approach her prospective customers. They were designing and tailoring email/social messaging to help open doors. They were also supporting small roundtable and presentation-style events for her customers/prospects with invitations and speakers.

Francesca was owning these events and campaigns. She was controlling the messaging and timing to her customers. She wasn't waiting on someone else to do it. At the end of the year, reporting showed that Francesca had a 24% higher pipeline build and 31% higher close ratio than the average salesperson across the country. Her targeted/tailored consistent messaging was making all the difference. She was her own campaign/event manager.

In summary:

> ➤ Consider yourself as your own Chief Marketing Officer.
> ➤ Know your customer base.
> ➤ Create highly focused target lists.
> ➤ Collaborate with your marketing team but own your initiatives.
> ➤ Monitor and report on your success sources.

PLAY 4.
IT'S WHERE THE MAGIC IS

LOOK FOR THE OLYMPIAN GOLD MEDAL CUSTOMER EXPERIENCE

I AM INCREDIBLY fortunate to have spent over two decades collaborating with founders and businesses that place customer experience at the very heart of their operations. One significant role I played was as the spokesperson for the Heartbeat program, an initiative aimed at cultivating a culture that prioritizes and shares exceptional customer experiences across the company. Remarkably, out of more than 450 global competitors, we were recognized as having the 'Best Customer Experience in the World' by a panel of 60 international judges - a stellar achievement that filled everyone involved with immense pride.

So, what constitutes excellent customer experience and why is it crucial? The answer lies in the very DNA of the business, influencing all aspects of its operations. It's a broad subject, a book in itself, so let's focus on the role of the salesperson in particular and consider the perspective of the customer.

Imagine you are tasked with procuring a product, service, or solution for your business. What do you expect from the salesperson you engage with? Likely, you're looking for:

- Early high-level information relevant to your needs to determine if further investigation is worthwhile.

- A genuine desire to understand your requirements and motivations.
- Effective communication skills: the ability to listen and articulate concisely.
- Insight and expertise in the field, offering new knowledge or confirming optimal solutions.
- Quick responses and consistent updates demonstrating their commitment to the task.
- Confidence in their ability to get things done.
- Helpful resources to support your internal presentations and progress.
- Consistency in delivering quality service.

After walking in the customer's shoes, ask yourself as the salesperson: "How else can I serve my customer? What additional value can I offer?" It's here that you might discover the magic you can bring to the table. Of course, you need to master the points listed above, but what about the unexpected? The surprising elements? Seek the unique magic that exceeds their expectations. Perhaps it's a personal touch relating to their work or personal life that makes the difference.

Executing these elements well enables you to forge robust business relationships that span years, built on a foundation of trust and faith in your ability to deliver – possibly blossoming into meaningful friendships.

Think of a hotel stay as an analogy. You expect the elevator to function, the room key to work, a neatly made bed, hot water for your shower, and a clean, tidy room. At this level, would you recommend the hotel to a friend or colleague? Probably not. But, what if, in addition to meeting these expectations, the concierge warmly greets you by name, assists you in securing a reservation at your favourite restaurant, and the staff is consistently cheerful, making you feel special? Now, you're more likely to enthusiastically recommend the hotel. This example illustrates that while meeting basic expectations is necessary, it's the extra level of service that sets you apart and encourages customers not only to continue their patronage but also to recommend your services.

As the Head of the IT Project Delivery team, James was delighted to grab a coffee with Client Director, Tim. The promises Tim made during the extensive sales process had been realized, and the solution that Tim sold, and the subsequent project rollout had been a success.

Sitting in the coffee shop, they started with a congratulatory discussion, which then shifted to a casual chat about sports. James mentioned that his football team had just won a State Championship over the weekend and even showed a photo on his phone of him scoring the winning shot. Tim was intrigued and said, "Send me that photo, the guys in the office would love to see it." Within seconds, the photo was in Tim's messages.

Two days later, as James sat at his desk in his office, a courier package arrived for him. He opened the padded envelope and found a framed acrylic block displaying his proud sporting moment. It came with a personalized note: "Thank you, James, for the hard work and effort on the project. This is a small token of thanks. - Tim." James was taken aback by this thoughtful gesture. He placed the frame on his desk, a memento of that triumphant moment. He called Tim to express his gratitude, mentioning that Tim shouldn't have gone to such lengths, but genuinely appreciating it. Such a heart-warming gesture!

James and Tim went on to maintain a business relationship over many years. Tim's personal interest and thoughtfulness went beyond the routine business norm, adding a bit of magic to the consistent delivery of reliable service.

In summary:

> Think as if you are the customer. Consider what they want and need, not just from the business aspect, but also individually.
> Act swiftly.
> Own the situation for them. Maintain a 'consider it done' attitude.
> Exhibit consistent reliability.
> Always contemplate, "What else can I do for them?"

RAPPORT

IN THE CAMBRIDGE dictionary, 'rapport' is defined as a 'good understanding of someone and an ability to communicate well with them'.

These attributes are fundamental for exceptional salespeople. Without them, sales can still occur; after all, it's not about being the most popular. Buyers often choose the best-fitting product or service, even if they are not fond of the salesperson. However, consistent success and becoming an invaluable asset to your organization requires feedback like: "she's fantastic to deal with", "I want him on our account", "she's a ten out of ten", "I highly recommend him". This level of commentary will harness the power of referrals and recommendations.

We've already discussed the necessity of understanding your customer, empathizing with their experience, the art of listening and asking incisive questions to uncover their desires and needs. Moreover, you need a genuine desire to comprehend them and how you and your business can help. This understanding goes beyond merely selling them your services. These are the sales personalities that consistently win business because customers trust their authenticity.

Subtly mirroring the customer's personality is a potent skill for building rapport. If they speak quickly and expressively, you can align your style. If they are introverted and deliberate in their thinking, you should slow down and soften your approach. People often feel more comfortable with those similar to themselves. You don't need to drastically alter your personality; you simply need to be aware of the customer's style, recognize it, and adapt your approach to resonate with them.

For instance, imagine you're an extrovert who enjoys being the vibrant, smiling, and energetic leader in the room. You quickly realize the customer is quite the opposite — quiet, reserved, speaking softly. You maintain your bright and confident persona but tone it down. You ask insightful questions and listen intently, reiterating your understanding to show your sincere attention. The customer will recognize your vibrant character, yet also notice your adaptability and eagerness to understand them. That's excellent rapport-building!

Anna is discussing a business solution with a prospective customer who needs reassurance that her business is sound, reliable, and trustworthy. Anna makes a call to a previous customer, Liz, and asks if she would mind grabbing a coffee or lunch with her and the prospect. The purpose being for Liz to share her story of implementation and ongoing support. Liz responds with, "Absolutely no problem, it's the least I can do based on the great service from you and the team."

The meeting takes place and Anna introduces commonalities between the customer and prospect's company. She asks Liz to walk through their story of dealing with Anna and her business. In doing so, Anna mirrors Liz's story to build rapport and make it easier for the prospect to envision their own successful engagement with Anna and her business.

Liz is effusive in her praise: "I can't speak highly enough of Anna's support, how our project was completed, and how good the ongoing support has been." What a powerful endorsement! Anna's rapport with Liz is evident and is a true demonstration of what the prospect can expect from her and the team. They are now more likely to choose Anna based on this recommendation.

Now, imagine the opposite. Anna isn't able to get a customer to vouch for her. Customers ignore her calls and messages seeking referrals. Why is that? It must be because she hasn't built sufficient rapport; they haven't been impressed with her service or her ability to consistently deliver. It could be that Anna feels it's out of her control and that it's the fault of other departments in the business that aren't delivering. While this might be true, it's crucial to remember that the customer should always perceive you as their champion. No excuses.

In summary:

- ➢ Build rapport by truly understanding your customer and demonstrating that understanding.
- ➢ Foster rapport through clear communication — listening, speaking, and writing effectively.
- ➢ Adapt your personality style, balanced to fit with the customer's style.
- ➢ Be genuinely motivated to learn about the customer.

AUTHENTICITY

THE CUSTOMER EXPERIENCE commences with their first impression of you. This impression could be formed from an email, an event, a phone call, or the moment you step into the room. It continues throughout your interactions, and like any relationship, it's not fixed. It shifts depending on how you engage over time. No pressure!

Respect is fundamental in all communications. How do you present yourself? Are you well-groomed, punctual, maintaining eye contact, and displaying genuine interest? Recalling an instance when someone didn't respect these basics isn't pleasant, right? Such individuals fall to the back of your "trustworthy people" list. Therefore, it's crucial to be present and open in all interactions.

Openness is a desirable trait. A sales meeting or call should feel as casual as a friendly conversation. Adopting an open, relaxed demeanour encourages the customer to respond similarly. Contrarily, if the salesperson appears nervous or defensive, it makes the customer close off. There's no need to play a superhero character. Authenticity is key. Focus on understanding the customer's needs and matching them with the right business solutions. A relaxed, open, and genuine approach enhances transparency and builds trust.

Solidifying trust depends on providing proof points for your proposals. Sharing relatable customer stories and references helps the customer evaluate your proposal and improves their experience. You are clearing their path of doubt by demonstrating your understanding of their situation.

Meeting your commitments is also key in fostering trust. Remember, you are the owner of the customer's experience. Even if your colleagues fail to respond quickly, you must hold yourself accountable. Clear, transparent communication, even when delivering unpleasant news, is crucial. As the saying goes, "good news can wait, bad news cannot." This transparency is often respected by customers, as long as they know you are working for their benefit.

Authenticity shines when you demonstrate calmness, confidence, and expertise in your subject matter. It is about finding common ground, making the listener comfortable, and guiding them in their decision-making process. Whether this comes naturally to you or if you need to practice, being genuinely authentic is a critical skill for successful selling.

Val is the CFO for a major healthcare provider. With tightening budgets and increased costs, the last thing he wants is poor support from vendors. After making a change from a long-term supplier due to increased costs and poor service, he responds to the new provider's customer experience survey and his new Account Manager, Vince.

"I'll score Vince a 10 out of 10 for customer service. His commitment to our business is exceptional. He's always available, gets back to us quickly, and when we have issues, I know he's on it for us. I can trust Vince to be there and offer us good advice. Compared to our previous Account Manager, who we couldn't get hold of and when we did, he didn't follow through, Vince is a breath of fresh air. It's hard to find good customer experience, but his authenticity shines through. He is a credit to your company. We look forward to doing more business with Vince and your company for many years."

We can see in this example how much value the customer, Val, places on the actions of the Account Manager, Vince. It's a mix of availability, responsiveness, and shared knowledge that leads to his 'authenticity shines through' comment. What's more, this level of service is clearly going to lead to more business and sales for Vince. That means Vince has a happy customer, a happy manager, and that pleasant feeling of success from helping the customer, while achieving his and the company's goals.

In summary:

- ➢ First and ongoing impressions count. Be aware of how you will come across in your appearance and communications to the customer. Be respectful and focused on them.
- ➢ Open up and be yourself – Lose the defensive aspects of self-consciousness; the meeting or call is about the customer, not you.
- ➢ Focus on how you can link to their interests and seek to help them.
- ➢ Meet your promises and take action on time. Clearly communicate progress.
- ➢ Speak with confidence, calmness, and display knowledge, always considering how you are connecting with the customer.

PLAY 5.
MIND YOUR MIND

SALES PSYCHOLOGY

YES! YOU'VE CAPTURED the big sale, your heart races as you stride home, a spring in your step and a song on your lips. Celebratory messages pop up on your phone, hailing from every corner of the company. You are the hero of the hour, and it feels magnificent. True, a bonus or commission may follow this victory, but it's the surge of accomplishment that gives you a real kick; a rush of dopamine, your brain's reward for hitting the mark. Life is good!

Now, contrast this elation with: "Oh no, this doesn't sound good". The customer's words lead to a sombre: "Sorry, we've chosen a different solution. We appreciate your efforts, and we'll consider you in the future". As you brace for the letdown, you hear these gut-wrenching words. Your heart plunges, your spirit shrivels; you dread breaking the news to your boss, your team. The world blurs as you focus solely on the customer's voice and the piercing disappointment.

Which scenario do we prefer? The first, unquestionably. However, in sales, you must buckle up for the roller coaster ride. These are two polar opposites on the emotional spectrum, experienced by salespeople with victories and defeats. Both are self-generated. Yes, by you! Both stem from the internal narrative you're consciously or subconsciously spinning. There's joy, excitement, and pride on one hand, and on the other, disappointment, anxiety, frustration, or even anger.

Winning is a marvellous feeling, much like the victorious athletes who claim, "We make winning a habit". Sales demand the same level of consistency and habit. It has to be second nature, replicable. Successful tactics should be identified, embedded in your memory and psyche, and repeated with unwavering positivity. Business sales aren't for the faint-hearted; you must wear your emotional armour, allowing rejection's arrows to glance off while you press forward. Everyone loses sales, and I mean everyone. Those who learn, adapt, and keep pressing on, however, are the ones who succeed.

We can always learn from wins and losses, adjusting for the next opportunity. If you foster this mindset, you will be constantly improving. You will feel disappointment when you lose, but you won't dwell there. You'll be onto the next prospect before long. Try to recall the deals won and lost a year ago in sales. It's challenging, isn't it? The ordinary, day-to-day one's blur in our memories. Therefore, don't dwell on losses. Keep your gaze forward.

Avoid excuses and negativity.

Be aware of when your mind ventures into negativity. Top-tier salespeople display an optimistic outlook, finding ways to attain their goals and take responsibility. They are not shrinking violets when the support from the business is insufficient. They demand more and voice genuine concerns without resorting to trivial excuses. High-performing salespeople will look for greener pastures if their valid concerns are consistently overlooked by upper management. However, remember that if grumblings and negativity are perceived as excuses for underperformance, a salesperson could face repercussions, including dismissal. One way to gauge your performance, setting personal ego aside, is to compare your results with the rest of the salesforce. Are you consistently in the top 10% or 20%? Congratulations! If not, it's time for a reality check on your work ethic, skills, and attitude. Seek feedback from a respected manager or coach. Ask your customers, too, but bear in mind that they may not wish to hurt your feelings.

Whenever you notice negative thoughts creeping into your consciousness, challenge the story/belief that's emerging. The Neuro-Linguistic Programming (NLP) 'Precision Model' is a highly effective tool if memorized and frequently used. This model consists of five types of negative thoughts/statements, each of which can be challenged.

1. **Universals** - Such as, "I'm always losing", "I'll never win", "Everything's going wrong". Challenge these thoughts by questioning, "Really, do I always lose? Or just sometimes?" "Is it true that I'll never win?" "Is absolutely everything going wrong or just some things?" This brings a more balanced perspective and reduces anxiety.

2. **"Should, shouldn't, must, can't"** - These are typically fearful "what if" statements about past or future events. Ask questions like, "How can I learn from what happened?" "What did I do well?" "What specifically could happen and how likely is that?" By addressing fear head-on, you see the situation for what it truly is, not worse.

3. **Verb** - Thoughts like "I'm scared" or "I'm tired". Challenge these by asking, "What specifically scares me?" "What's happening in my body?" "What thoughts are leading me to feel this way?" This offers a deeper understanding and a fresh perspective.

4. **Noun** - Related to people and places, like "He's useless", "I hate this place". Challenge these by asking, "Is he really useless all the time?" "Is this place always awful?"

5. **"Too"** statements - "It's too hard", "We are too small". Challenge these by asking, "Compared to what exactly?"

Regular practice of these challenges will aid in managing negative thinking before it escalates or loops into a depressive state. Particularly in new business sales, where rejection can be high, it's important to equip yourself with mental resilience tools. Your job is to bring on brand new accounts and achieve the targets set by the company. They want winners who can deliver results. You will be lauded; placed on a pedestal when you do. You are the Top Gun! But only for a moment, as the next weeks, months, quarters targets lay ahead. That is the thrill, the motivation, the dopamine rush; the fact that your worth is always tied to your next sales performance.

In summary:

➤ You are the architect of your emotions when you win and lose.
➤ Learn from wins and losses - constant growth leads to a sense of achievement.
➤ Watch out for excuses and negativity.
➤ Adopt and regularly practice mental resilience tools like the Precision Model.

THE MOTIVATION OF GOALS

HAVE YOU EVER found yourself struggling to articulate your goals when asked, "What are your aspirations?" A quick, generic response might slip from your lips — "happiness," "health," "success." It's an easy cover-up, a way to evade the probing question that requires deep contemplation. But if the inquirer presses, "So, what are your precise goals, your immediate and long-term desires?" you are compelled to deliberate. How would you respond?

Many are challenged by this deeper query. It's a profound self-reflection question, pushing us to examine our life's motivations: what genuinely matters to us? What kindles our motivation today, tomorrow, or months from now? What propels us to make those sales calls, engage in research, rebound from losses, and double down after victories?

Here's a poignant anecdote of Olympian swimmer Michael Phelps, who clinched a world record-breaking 8 Gold medals at the Beijing Olympics. Phelps, the most decorated Olympian in history, with a total of 28 medals — 23 gold, idolized Australian swimming legend Ian Thorpe. When Thorpe expressed scepticism about Phelps's goal, Phelps used it as fuel. He clipped the newspaper article, pinning it to his locker as a daily reminder to defy doubters.

That's an exemplary illustration of a laser-focused, tenacious goal. Phelps indeed won the 8 Gold medals, etching his name in history.

While the parallel between business sales and Olympian feats might seem strained, the crux remains the same. If your goal drives you sufficiently, you'll put in the work and then some to succeed. This drive could fuel one sale or hundreds. Identifying the internal force that motivates you to persevere is essential.

Once you find that motivating force, the mental aspect of selling becomes like powering through water in a speedboat; waves splashing against the hull, swiftly vanishing in your wake. The effort, creativity, rejections, and victories don't deter you; instead, they form part of your journey towards your goals.

Understanding Goal Setting

Your mind is your most potent weapon. The brain's occipital lobe, constituting 20% of its overall capacity, is responsible for visualizing scenes. For instance, envision a polar bear in pink pyjamas, climbing a tree. Vivid, isn't it? This simple exercise demonstrates the power of the occipital lobe and visualization. Studies reveal that creative individuals display high Theta electrical brain wave activity — the waves that we employ during daydreaming or the drifting state before sleep. By harnessing this skill of visualization, combined with strategy and persistence, you will be unstoppable in your pursuit of goals.

Insights from authors like Tim Ferriss, known for his book 'The 4 Hour Work Week', can be incredibly beneficial in goal setting. Ferriss suggests breaking down goals into three categories:

Who you want to be?

What do you want to have?

What do you want to do?

He added to this a cost factor for each goal, so you have a budget to work to also. In my own simplistic modelling of the tool, it looks like this EG:

Goal Type	I will be	I will have	I will do	Cost per year	Next action	By when
Holiday			Rome in July with family. See the Coliseum, Pantheon. Trevi Fountain.	$12000	1) Book Leave 2) Book flight 3) Book Hotel	1) May 1 2) May 2 3) May 2
Achieve	No.1 Salesperson nationally for Q2			$0	1) Create 5 times target in real prospects 2) Close 120% target	1) April 20 2) 30 June
Finance		$12000 in savings		$0	1) Transfer to savings, bonus / commissions as they come in	1) monthly

Dave Allen, author of the bestseller 'Getting Things Done,' emphasizes the brain's capability for ideation rather than task completion. He cites cognitive science research, which proves that our brain can only manage four things concurrently. Therefore, it's crucial to organize your thoughts and clearly define tasks to prevent stress and anxiety. In the context of goal-setting, the act of brainstorming who you aspire to be, what you wish to possess, and what you hope to achieve, coupled with visualization of each goal and outlining the necessary actions, liberates your mind. Simultaneously, this process consciously and subconsciously instils purpose and determination, fortifying your pursuit of sales targets. Utilizing pictures, photos, or articles, much like in Phelps's story, can provide additional motivational stimuli.

Don't hesitate to give it a go. Sip a cup of coffee or tea — whatever stirs your creativity — and ponder on your true desires. If it's helpful, engage a coach or family member in this brainstorming session to bounce ideas around. Activate your motivations. Understand your wants.

Siobhan, an Account Manager for a global health food distributor, is feeling overwhelmed. Her sales results are at only 40%, and she's six months into the year. This situation is causing her distress. She finds it difficult to make calls and lacks confidence in front of customers. Despite working hard every day, the results aren't forthcoming. It feels like walking in a fog with no clear sight of a breakthrough.

Sandra, the Area Manager, meets with Siobhan to discuss her results and progress. Sandra listens, absorbs the information, and asks Siobhan in a calm, inquisitive voice, "What are your goals this year, Siobhan? Not just work-related but outside of work too?" Siobhan looks up at Sandra, ponders, and says, "I just want to do well and be successful." Sandra probes further, "That's good, but what do you genuinely want? What would make this year exciting? That if you achieve your sales results, you can do xyz. What is that?" Siobhan leans back and thinks again, "Well, I'd love to treat my family with a trip to Disneyland. We've never been, and it would be fantastic to go and have some fun." "That's great," Sandra responds as she smiles, nods, and reiterates the exciting goal. "So, a Disneyland treat is No.1. What else?" "I'd love to earn a formal educational certificate in nutrition. It will bolster my customer interactions and knowledge. It would be a personal achievement. If I perform well and earn bonuses, I can pay for the course."

"Great," Sandra replies, "you now have two exciting goals for the year. I'll add an additional incentive. If you achieve your numbers for the remaining months, we'll contribute towards the funding for the nutrition course. Just provide me with the details." She then asks, "So, what are you going to do about these goals? What are your next steps?"

Siobhan's energy has noticeably changed; her head is lifted, her shoulders are squared, and she's animated and smiling. "I'm going to research Disneyland and find out the times and costs for the holidays. I'll place a picture of it front and center on my laptop screen as a reminder of what I'm aiming for. I'll do the same with the nutrition course. I'm excited to get started!"

"Fantastic," Sandra responds. "Whatever help I or anyone can provide, let us know. We want to ensure your success. Let's check in each week. I can't wait to see the Disney photos!"

In this interaction, Siobhan rejuvenates her spirit and energy by focusing on an exciting experience she can share with her family. She has also identified a deep satisfaction in wanting to grow as a person through the nutrition course. These goals align with the 'what will I do' and 'what will I have' categories. That clarity of focus, coupled with visualization and the accompanying emotion, have cleared the fog. When days are tough or energy is low, having these motivational goals to push forward and go the extra step will be crucial.

In summary:

- ➢ Take the time to identify your dreams and goals.
- ➢ Discover what you genuinely want to achieve, do, have, and be.
- ➢ Use visualization, a powerful tool.
- ➢ Get it out of your head and onto paper or digital format in an action plan. Clear your thoughts.
- ➢ Set timelines and action steps in place, and regularly review and calibrate them.

DISCIPLINE

"DISCIPLINE EQUALS FREEDOM" is a poignant phrase attributed to Jocko Willink, a former Navy Seal Commander, author, and consultant. In his youth, Jocko admits to being somewhat uncontrolled, veering off course. However, the structure provided by the Navy allowed him to cultivate focus, purpose, and, ultimately, freedom. This discipline facilitated his growth as a warrior, leader, mentor, and person. The phrase itself, juxtaposing two seemingly opposite concepts, commands attention.

One might typically view discipline and freedom as contraries. Discipline could evoke memories of lengthy school days, rigid adherence to rules, a coach's insistence on defensive tactics, or parental reprimands for leaving the dinner table. Freedom, on the contrary, meant the absence of rules and the liberty to carve one's path. Nevertheless, unless one possesses the inner resolve to resist the voice that encourages complacency, success will be elusive in life's key arenas: financial, social, health, and spiritual. These arenas offer the freedom to do the things you desire and be the person you aspire to be.

A sales framework demands discipline:

- **Know and/or set targets/Key Performance Indicators (KPIs).** These need to focus on a) the creation of pipeline opportunities and b) actual sales results. Companies will always set targets for you. However, don't take these as is. Consider your financial aspirations and recognition. If the company's target for you is $10,000 per month in new revenue, perhaps set your personal target at $12,000 per month to finance the visionary goals you've set, such as a family holiday to Rome, a down payment on a new home, or school fees.

- **Measure performance against targets.** Maintaining the discipline to consistently monitor how you are tracking to your targets, and having an honest view of performance will motivate subsequent actions. Comparing your performance to the rest of the team can stimulate a healthy competitive spirit. Your Sales Manager, I'd expect, will also regularly check in with you. Knowing exactly where you stand and what you need to do can instil confidence in your dedication to success.

- **Learn, learn, learn.** If you believe you have all the answers, congratulations on your confidence. However, as Socrates stated: "The only true wisdom is in knowing you know nothing." Continuous learning and growth will keep you at the forefront of your field. Keep in mind, nothing stands still. Competitors are always seeking an edge. Enhancing your knowledge not only offers a better chance to succeed but also creates solid relationships with customers.

- **Be mindful of your behaviour.** Organisations, and even departments within organisations, have different cultures, dictated by their size and leadership. Being aware of your customers' culture increases your chances of success. Discipline manifests in various forms within these cultures.

- **Punctuality for meetings is an easy start.** Aim to arrive a little early and always ensure you have enough travel time. If you're going to be late, send a message in advance. This consideration will be appreciated, as the other person(s) can use that time for other tasks. Being consistently punctual enhances your reputation and indicates respect, our next point of discussion.

- **Respect for others should be a standard.** Communication, both written and verbal, should reflect understanding and empathy. Avoid engaging in negative tirades or gossip. If you have a legitimate issue with someone's work or behaviour, raise it with management and stay focused on your task at hand.

- **Dress appropriately.** Some cultures in business sales might require smart casual attire, others a strictly business suit. Be aware of both your company's and your customers' dress codes. If you're meeting at a customer's office or out for lunch, consider their dress code. It doesn't require a one-hour strategy session; just a brief thought to ensure you blend in as much as possible. If your appearance is scruffy, it can reflect a lack of discipline and be interpreted as laziness or untrustworthiness.

- **Allocate time for introspection.** Amid the daily hustle, it's vital to reserve quiet moments for reflection. Comedian Billy Connolly once advised, "Every day, take time out to just sit and take in the moment If you're having a coffee, focus on the taste, the creamy froth, zone in be aware..." By doing this, you free up cognitive space to invite creative thoughts. A mere ten minutes each day can be incredibly beneficial, especially if you can change your surroundings during this time.

Remember, discipline equates to freedom. Adherence to these principles does not constrict but liberates you to be the best version of yourself, both personally and professionally.

It's the end of the year, and Roy sits down in front of his laptop. He has allocated a few hours to reflect on the past six months' performance. He evaluates what's worked and what hasn't, considering what he could have done differently to achieve his personal 110% target goal. Although he hit 100% and has been successful in the business, he fell short of his personal target. This 10% difference in the bonus means he's short on funds for a deposit on a new car. Nonetheless, he's optimistic and reassures himself, "I'll make it up."

Next, Roy outlines his opportunity creation and sales targets for the upcoming six months, breaking them down into weekly, monthly, and total targets. He reviews his pipeline and aligns the deals with the month he expects them to close based on his gut feelings. He identifies gaps in certain months and calculates the amount of opportunity creation he'll need to fill these gaps. Roy then reviews his list of top prospects and formulates an action plan.

He also notes that sales were 50% lower in one of his lines of business. He realizes that a marginal increase in this quota could earn him the extra 10% bonus for his car. Aware that his product and competitor knowledge in this area are lacking, he schedules training with the product manager and arranges to shadow the company's highest seller of the solution on a sales call. He's determined to improve his knowledge and gain more confidence when engaging with customers in this area.

Roy conducts this in-depth review every quarter. It's a discipline that helps him understand exactly what he needs to do to improve and meet his targets.

In summary:

> By being disciplined in your actions and behaviours, you will create opportunities and achieve results, providing you with clarity of purpose as well as financial security, better relationships, health, and personal growth.

> Dive in, create habits that make discipline second nature.

> Discipline requires willpower and drive. No excuses—it's all up to you.

CONCLUSION

FANTASTIC! WE'VE DELVED into the how and what of successful B2B selling. Like all enlightening insights, you'll extract the golden nuggets to enrich your toolkit. I trust you've uncovered the 'don't' in the 'What You Already Know and Don't' section of the book. Even if it's not from the lessons of the plays, one thing we all agree on is that we can't fully grasp the intricacies of every customer. That's the adventure—your capacity to be curious, to comprehend their business, and to understand the individual's desires and needs. If you can forge these connections, you're paving your road to success.

Define and master the formula for success in Play 1. Recognize the onus is squarely on you to fuel your own sales success. From groundwork and strategizing to scouting potential clients and effectively communicating with both prospective and ongoing customers. You helm the ship, navigating through calms and storms, persistently charting the course forward.

In Play 2, we emphasize the pivotal role of skilling up to achieve victory. The undeniable value of questioning techniques, active listening, note-taking, and translating those insights into compelling proposals and presentations that make the customer say, "you really understood our business". The more adept you become, the greater asset you are to your enterprise and the client. In the classic 'The Richest Man In Babylon', there is a line: "Be invaluable to your employer". That's a position to aspire to. It grants you assurance, acknowledgment, and prospects for growth, whether within your current business or when another door opens.

You can't soar solo! In Play 3, the essence of teamwork takes centre stage. Engaging specialists, operations, partners, customers, managers. Recall a profound success that resonates emotionally. Got it? Now, reflect on those who contributed with you. Success achieved by collaboration amplifies its resonance, the memory of the experience. Combining your expertise with your team's knowledge and abilities can exponentially increase your odds of success.

Where would we be without our customers? Absolutely adrift. In Play 4, we chase the zenith of customer service excellence. Cultivate this habit, focusing on genuine empathy and understanding of the individual. You have to provide the service, consistently, build the trust that you are their go to person, in their corner. The magic is in the beyond this. How can you turn the expected into something more for them. Relationships for many years are formed from such actions. Be true, authentic. We feel good when we do good for others.

B2B sales isn't a leisurely stroll. It resembles a tightrope walk—juggling today's deals with the unforeseeable future. Every salesperson knows that sensation—eyeballing a thinning pipeline and thinking, "oh oh! it's looking sparse". In Play 5, we explore nurturing a proactive, motivating mindset, one that deflects arrows of negativity. Discipline in planning, daily tasks, and goal setting creates a trustworthy foundation. The beauty in sales is that cycles repeat. I've lost count of the lost deals that, in later years, turned into wins—the client recalling the professionalism and strong bids from before. As Arnold Schwarzenegger said, "the secret to life is to be useful to others and to work your ass off". In B2B sales, you're offering solutions that elevate a customer's world. How hard you work your ass off to get there is up to you. That option is always there though, no matter how tough a day may seem. Isn't that a good thought!

Finally thank you sincerely for taking the time to read this book. It means so much. I wish you every success in life and career. Enjoy the wins, learn from the losses and then enjoy the wins again. They are always in front of you.

ACKNOWLEDGEMENTS

THIS BOOK WOULD not have been possible without the personality traits of wanting to be creative and being driven to share lessons I have learned with anyone interested enough to listen. Perhaps we come into this world with a pre-determined personality. However, for sure we are moulded and curated from our childhood learnings and observations of those closest to us. We adapt and find our place in the family unit and the wider community. For these positive traits and lessons that I draw on every day, I thank my Mum and Dad: Andrew Leo, Rose Marie and brothers Graham and Derek Tighe.

Testing your writing with friends, colleagues and best-selling authors can be a little daunting. However, it is a vital step towards putting out the best possible version of the work. Thank you to everyone who took the time to read the manuscript and offer advice and suggestions for improvement. The feedback was invaluable. Special shout out to: Joseph Michelli, James Allen, Bill Agelidis, Michael Davies, Oisin O'Callaghan, Nigel Bouche, Luke Clifton, Peter James.

A massive thank you to my work colleagues and customers, who teach me so much about sales and customer service every day. I have been fortunate to work with Macquarie Technology Group for over 23 years and prior to this, an amazing sales management team at ntl in the UK. A thirty year plus career in business sales will see a plethora of interactions with fellow staff and customers. There are of course too many people to mention here but every single person has had an impact. They helped answer the never-ending quest towards: 'What we don't know'. For the lessons and companionship along the way – Thank you.

REFERENCES

Play 1 Chapter - Prospecting for Appointments and Opportunities
Glengarry Glen Ross (film), Zupnik Enterprises, 1992.

Play 1 Chapter - Pick Up the Phone and Ring
Jeb Blount, Fanatical Prospecting, Wiley, 2015.

Play 2 Chapter – Skill Up to Win
Chris Voss, Tahl Raz Never split the difference, HarperCollins, 2018.

Play 2 Chapter – Active Listening
Jim Kwik, https://www.jimkwik.com/podcasts/kwik-brain-002-im-prove-your-memory-now/, march 28, 2017.
Pon Staff. https://www.pon.harvard.edu/daily/negotia-tion-skills-daily/is-your-negotiating-style-holding-you-back-nb/, Harvard Law School, June 15, 2014.

Play 2 Chapter – Note Taking
Hermann Ebbinghaus, The forgetting curve. 1885.
Richard Branson, Losing my virginity, Virgin Books, 1995.

Play 2 Chapter – It's All About the Product Right?
Glengarry Glen Ross (film), Zupnik Enterprises, 1992
Leonardo DiCaprio, Wolf of Wall Street, 2014

Play 2 Chapter – Objections, Contract Negotiations & Execution
James Allen (Bain & Company). The Perfect Analogy.

Play 5 Chapter – Mind your Mind
John Thomas Grinder Jr, Richard Bandler, Neuro Linguistic Programming, The Precision Model.
Michael Phelps, Olympic swimmer, USA.
Ian Thorpe, Olympic swimmer, Australia.

Play 5 Chapter – The Motivation of Goals
Tim Ferriss, The 4-hour work week, Crown publishing, 2007.
Dave Allen, Getting things done, New York: Penguin Putnam, 2001.

Play 5 Chapter – Discipline
Jocko Willink, Discipline equals freedom. Pan Macmillan, 2017.

Conclusion
Arnold Schwarzenegger, Tim Ferris podcast, #696 3rd Oct 2023.
George S Clayson, The Richest Man in Babylon. Penguin Books, 1926.

Index

Printed in the USA
CPSIA information can be obtained
at www.ICGtesting.com
LVHW041936050524
779283LV00006B/128